T0349853

märklin
MODERNE

jovis

DAM DEUTSCHES ARCHITEKTURMUSEUM

mR moderne REGIONAL

KARIN BERKEMANN
DANIEL BARTETZKO
(HG./EDS.)

märklin
MODERNE

VOM BAU ZUM BAUSATZ
UND ZURÜCK

FROM ARCHITECTURE
TO ASSEMBLY KIT AND BACK AGAIN

jovis

MODELLE UND BAUTEN
MODELS AND BUILDINGS

ANHANG
APPENDIX

DANIEL BARTETZKO UND KARIN BERKEMANN
MODERNEREGIONAL, KURATOREN DER AUSSTELLUNG

Vorwort

DANIEL BARTETZKO UND KARIN BERKEMANN
MODERNEREGIONAL, EXHIBITION CURATORS

Foreword

Im Hobbykeller der Wirtschafts-wunderzeit drehte die Dampflok ihre Runden nicht nur zwischen Fachwerkhäusern – auf der Modellbahnplatte gab es immer auch die Architekturmoderne. Flugdach, Rasterfassade und Glaskuppel fanden sich in den Katalogen der Häuschenhersteller wie Faller, Vollmer oder Kibri oft schon früher als romantisierende Altbauten. Wer 4,75 Mark und ein paar Groschen für eine Tube Plastikkleber übrig hatte, konnte sich seine eigene „Villa im Tessin" leisten. 1961 präsentierten Hermann und Edwin Faller stolz diesen inzwischen zum Kultobjekt gereiften Bausatz. Das reale Vorbild, ein futuristisches Wohnhaus in der Nähe des Gotthardtunnels, hatte die Brüder gleich doppelt inspiriert. Sie entwickelten das tausendfach ver-kaufte Modell, bei ihrem Firmensitz in Gütenbach entstand parallel eine ähnliche Villa in groß. Nicht minder kuriose Geschichten stecken auch hinter einem gläsernen Turmcafé, einer umkämpften Stadtkirche oder einem ostmodernen Hochhaus. Entlang solcher Beispiele folgt märklinMODERNE erstmals dem Weg der Architekturmoderne auf die Modellbahnplatte. Und zurück. Den Namen Märklin haben wir uns dabei nur geliehen, denn es geht hier nicht um das „fahrende Material". Doch Märklin ist längst zum Synonym für die Modellbahn im Allgemei-nen geworden. Die Ausstellung ist ein Projekt des Online-Magazins moderneREGIONAL, das seit 2014 ehrenamtlich täglich frische Beiträge und vierteljährlich Themenhefte rund um die Architekturmoderne veröffent-licht. Beide, die virtuelle Plattform wie die analoge Ausstellung, wollen

In the hobby rooms of the post-war economic boom, steam engines did not just wind their laps between half-timbered houses—architectural modernism was also always present on model railway boards. In catalogs by miniature producers such as Faller, Vollmer, or Kibri, floating roofs, grid-like facades, and glass cupolas often appeared even before roman-ticized historic buildings. For 4.75 German marks and a few pennies for a tube of plastic glue, you could afford your own "Villa in Ticino." This model kit, which has since achieved cult status, was proudly presented by Hermann and Edwin Faller in 1961. The real building on which it was modeled, a futuristic home near the Gotthard tunnel, actually inspired the brothers twice. They developed the model, of which thousands were sold, and near their office in Güten-bach they built a similar, life-size villa. There are equally strange and funny stories behind a glass tower cafe, a disputed city church, and an East German modernist high-rise. Using such examples, märklin-MODERNE examines architectural modernism's journey onto model railway boards—and back again—for the first time. We only borrowed the name Märklin, as it is not about the "rolling stock." However, for a long time Märklin has been a synonym for the model railway in general. The exhibition is a project by the online magazine moderneREGIO-NAL, which has published new daily articles and quarterly periodicals about architectural modernism on a voluntary basis since 2014. Both the virtual platform and the analog exhibition seek to convey the value of post-war architecture and thus con-

Hoch- und Fachwerkhäuser traulich
vereint im Faller-Modellbaukatalog
1973/74
High-rises and half-timbered houses
are presented side-by-side in the
Faller modelmaking catalog from
1973/74

die Baukunst der Nachkriegszeit in
ihren Werten vermitteln und damit
zu ihrem Erhalt beitragen. märklin-
MODERNE weckt dafür spielerisch
schöne Erinnerungen an eine Zeit,
als moderne Bauten wie selbstverständlich zur selbst gebastelten
Miniaturwelt gehörten. Es ist uns

eine Ehre und eine Freude, für den
Start der Ausstellung im Deutschen
Architekturmuseum (DAM), Frankfurt
einen kundigen Partner gefunden zu
haben. Zugleich sehen wir es als großes Privileg, die Präsentation parallel
in einer Inkunabel der klassischen
Moderne, in der architekturgalerie

tribute to its preservation. märklin-
MODERNE playfully brings back
pleasant memories of a time in which
modern buildings were a natural part
of self-assembled miniature worlds. It
is an honor and a pleasure for us that
the German Architecture Museum
(DAM) has agreed to partner with us

for the start of the exhibition. At the
same time, we see it as a great privilege to be able to show the exhibition
simultaneously in one of the van-
guards of classical modernism, the
architekturgalerie am weißenhof e. V.,
Stuttgart, after which the exhibition
will travel throughout Germany. This

am weißenhof e. V. in Stuttgart, zeigen zu können, um anschließend bundesweit zu wandern. Das Projekt bereichern Otto Schweitzer und C. Julius Reinsberg mit einem eigens erstellten Dokumentarfilm, dessen Finanzierung durch ein Crowdfunding im Herbst 2017 sichergestellt werden konnte.

Im ersten Teil des vorliegenden Katalogs führen – nach einleitenden Vor- und Grußworten – Fachbeiträge, Interviews und ein Fotoessay durch die Welt des modernen Modellbaus. Der zweite Abschnitt stellt die acht ausgewählten Modelle mit ihren realen Vorbildern und Nachfolgern in Wort und Bild vor. Unser Dank gilt hierbei den versierten Autorinnen und Autoren aus Architektur und (Kunst-)Geschichte: Oliver Elser, Dina Dorothea Falbe, Teresa Fankhänel, Christian Holl, Ralf Liptau, Matthias Ludwig, Verena Pfeiffer-Kloss, C. Julius Reinsberg und Jörg Schilling – kongenial ergänzt durch die präzisen Architekturfotografien von Hagen Stier, die treffenden Interviewbilder von Andreas Beyer, das stilsichere Layout von Jutta Drewes und dessen fachkundige Weiterführung im Berliner JOVIS Verlag. Für die Interviews öffneten der Faller-„Hausarchitekt"

Leopold Messmer, der Plakatkünstler Klaus Staeck und der Architekturkritiker Falk Jaeger ihre Häuser und Kellerkisten. Bei unseren Ausstellungspartnern, bei Archiven und Firmen, bei ehemalig und bleibend Modellbegeisterten, bei den Leserinnen und Lesern von moderneREGIONAL, bei den Unterstützerinnen und Unterstützern des Crowdfundings, im Freundes- und Familienkreis sind wir auf viel Offenheit, Freundlichkeit und Hilfe gestoßen. Nicht zuletzt gilt unser Dank der Wüstenrot Stiftung, deren großzügige Förderung dieses Projekt erst möglich gemacht hat.

project is enriched by a documentary created by Otto Schweitzer and C. Julius Reinsberg, whose funding was ensured by a crowdfunding campaign in fall 2017.

Following the introductory forewords and greetings, the first part of this catalog contains essays, interviews, and a photo essay which guide the reader through the world of modern modelmaking. The second section presents photos and texts about eight selected models, the real buildings on which they were modeled, and their successors. We would like to thank the knowledgeable authors from architecture and (art) history: Oliver Elser, Dina Dorothea Falbe, Teresa Fankhänel, Christian Holl, Ralf Liptau, Matthias Ludwig, Verena Pfeiffer-Kloss, C. Julius Reinsberg, and Jörg Schilling. These texts are ideally complemented by precise architecture photography by Hagen Stier, fitting interview photographs by Andreas Beyer, a stylish layout by Jutta Drewes, and the competent realization of this project by JOVIS Verlag in Berlin. For the interviews, Faller "house architect" Leopold Messmer, poster artist Klaus Staeck, and architecture critic Falk Jaeger opened their homes and storage

boxes. We received a great deal of openness, friendliness, and help from our exhibition partners, at archives and organizations, from former and current model enthusiasts, from the readers of moderneREGIONAL, from the supporters of our crowdfunding campaign, and from our friends and families. Last but not least, we would like to thank the Wüstenrot Stiftung, whose generous funding made this project possible.

PETER CACHOLA SCHMAL, DIREKTOR DAM
OLIVER ELSER, KURATOR DAM

Vorwort

PETER CACHOLA SCHMAL, DAM DIRECTOR
OLIVER ELSER, DAM CURATOR

Foreword

Die Architektur der Nachkriegsmoderne ist mit einem Stigma behaftet. Immer wieder wird behauptet, sie sei von weiten Teilen der Bevölkerung nie akzeptiert worden. „Und wir nennen diesen Schrott auch noch schön", so der Titel einer wütenden Abrechnung, die der Schriftsteller Martin Mosebach im Jahr 2010 in der Frankfurter Allgemeinen Zeitung veröffentlichte. Die Öffentlichkeit, so der Vorwurf Mosebachs, leide seit Jahrzehnten unter den selbstherrlichen Architekten, die nun auch noch von verblendeten Denkmalpflegern dabei unterstützt würden, ihr Versagen zu unangreifbaren Monumenten zu verbrämen.

Wir sind uns bewusst, dass die Gründungsgeschichte des Deutschen Architekturmuseums (DAM) als deutsche Filiale der Postmodernedebatte viel dazu beigetragen hat, die Nachkriegsmoderne ins schale Licht des „Bauwirtschaftsfunktionalismus" zu rücken, wie der erste DAM-Direktor Heinrich Klotz die Epoche einmal vernichtend charakterisiert hat. Doch in diesen Jahren wilder Diskussionen wurden nicht nur, ein wenig abseits vom postmodernen Getöse, wichtige Nachlässe von Architekten der Nachkriegsjahre ans DAM geholt, wie etwa von Lucy Hillebrand oder Erich Schelling. Es fanden auch

Moderne auf „Stelzen": das Faller-Modell „Geschäftshausblock Helvetia"
Modernity on "stilts": the Faller model "Helvetia commercial block"

Post-war modern architecture is stigmatized. It has been claimed over and over that it has never been accepted by large portions of the population. This was reflected in an enraged piece entitled "And we even call this junk attractive" by Martin Mosebach, which was published in 2010 in the Frankfurter Allgemeine Zeitung. According to Mosebach's claims, the public has suffered for decades under self-important architects who are now even being supported by deluded monument preservationists in their quest to dress up their failures as unassailable monuments.

We are well aware that the history of the founding of the German Architecture Museum (DAM) as a German agency of the postmodernism debate significantly contributed to the casting of post-war modernism in the stale light of "construction industry functionalism," as the first DAM director, Heinrich Klotz, once scathingly described the era. However, in these years of wild discussions, somewhat removed from the postmodern racket, important legacies of post-war architects such as Lucy Hillebrand or Erich Schelling were brought to DAM. Exhibitions also took place which concentrated on the extremely fascinating question of how one could actually prove this alleged dissatisfaction with contemporary architecture.

The project märklinMODERNE represents a further such litmus test of public opinion. We hope that it will yield a result similar to the great popular success of the exhibition SOS Brutalism, which was also conducted in cooperation with the Wüstenrot Stiftung. The allegedly rejected

Die – inzwischen fast vollständig abgerissene – Frankfurter Oberfinanzdirektion (1955, Hans Köhler) im Modell (1952/53, 1960) aus dem Archiv des Deutschen Architekturmuseums (DAM), Frankfurt am Main
A model (1952/53, 1960) of the Oberfinanzdirektion in Frankfurt (1955, Hans Köhler)—the original has been nearly completely demolished—from the archive of the German Architecture Museum (DAM), Frankfurt am Main

Ausstellungen statt, die sich der hochgradig spannenden Frage widmeten, wie man die Unzufriedenheit an der Architektur der unmittelbaren Gegenwart eigentlich nachweisen kann.

Mit dem Projekt märklinMODERNE findet nun wieder ein solcher Lackmustest der öffentlichen Wertschätzung statt – wir hoffen mit einem ähnlichen Ergebnis, wie wir es bereits am großen Publikumserfolg der Ausstellung SOS Brutalismus beobachten konnten, die ebenfalls in Kooperation mit der Wüstenrot Stiftung stattfand: Die vermeintlich abgelehnte Architektur der Nachkriegsjahrzehnte stößt auf ein riesengroßes Interesse, gerade bei einem Publikum, das nicht zu den üblichen Kulturkonsumenten zählt. Die Brutalismus-Ausstellung hatte, das besagt die harte Statistik der verkauften Eintrittskarten, einen höheren Anteil an Besuchern, die nicht im Besitz einer Museums-Jahreskarte sind. Nun stellt sich dank der Recherche von moderneREGIONAL auch noch heraus, dass ein bisher eher belächelter, überwiegend männlicher Teil der Bevölkerung, der im Hobbykeller seinen Kontrollfantasien am Steuerpult einer Modelleisenbahn nachging, dass diese nach vulgär-

psychologischen Maßstäben durchaus suspekte Subspezies ein geradezu avantgardistisches Verhältnis zur Architektur ihrer Zeit gepflegt hat. Steckt in dieser notwendigen kulturgeschichtlichen Aufdeckungsleistung, die von moderneREGIONAL betrieben wurde, mehr als nur eine Fußnote zur Rezeptionsgeschichte der Moderne? Wir meinen: Ja! Wir sind froh, mit moderneREGIONAL einen Ausstellungspartner gewonnen zu haben, der über das Talent verfügt, auf unerwarteten Gebieten neues Material zur Moderne und Nachkriegsmoderne aufzustöbern. Wer hätte gedacht, wie viel uns die Spritzgussformen der Schwarzwälder Faller-Fabrik über unsere Vergangenheit erzählen können? Die andere Seite aber ist genauso wichtig: Deswegen ist es gut, dass der eingangs erwähnte Martin Mosebach als Autor für das Ausstellungsprojekt zur neuen Frankfurter Altstadt gewonnen werden konnte, das der freie Kurator Philipp Sturm für den Herbst 2018 vorbereitet. Teile dieser Altstadt werden übrigens ebenfalls als Modelleisenbahn-Häuser von der Firma Faller hergestellt. Die Baugeschichte im Maßstab 1:87 birgt noch manche Überraschungen.

architecture of the post-war decades is of great interest, especially for audiences who are not the usual cultural consumers. The hard statistics of the ticket sales for the brutalism exhibition showed that the majority of the visitors to the exhibition did not have an annual pass to the museum. Owing to research by moderneREGIONAL, it has now also emerged that a hitherto rather ridiculed, predominantly male section of the population who lived out their control fantasies at the controls of a model railway in their hobby cellar, representing a rather suspicious subspecies by vulgar psychological standards, cultivated a downright avant-garde relationship to the architecture of their era. Is there more than just a footnote to the history of the reception of modernism in the absolutely necessary cultural-historical research work undertaken by moderneREGIONAL? We think so! We are pleased to have gained an exhibition partner, moderneREGIONAL, which possesses the talent to unearth new material about modernism and post-war modernism in unexpected areas. Who would have thought that the injection form molds

of the Black Forest Faller factory could tell us so much about our past?

The other side is, however, equally important. For this reason it is good that we were able to win Martin Mosebach, mentioned at the beginning of this text, as an author for the exhibition project about the new Frankfurt historical city center which is being prepared by independent curator Philipp Sturm for the fall of 2018. Parts of this historical center were in fact also produced as model railway buildings by Faller. Architectural history on a scale of 1:87 harbors quite a few surprises.

Grußwort

Greeting

Die architekturgalerie am weißenhof e. V., die 1982 in Stuttgart gegründet wurde und seither etwa 175 Ausstellungen gezeigt hat, sieht ihre Aufgabe in der Vermittlung von Architektur in allen Medien, so auch dem Modell. Modelle von gebauter, geplanter oder fiktiver Architektur begleiten die Geschichte der Architektur seit der Antike. Sie sollten den Bauherren eine Anschauung des Baus vermitteln und dienten auch als Vorlage zum Weiterbau. Seit dem 15. Jahrhundert wurden Modelle als repräsentatives Darstellungsobjekt und erweitertes proportionales Planungsinstrument bei größeren Bauvorhaben zur Regel. Seither werden sie auch von der Kritik begleitet, nicht die Wirklichkeit abzubilden, sondern die Betrachter zu täuschen.

Die Modelle der Ausstellung märklinMODERNE sind anders zu bewerten als solche „normalen" Architekturmodelle. Sie sind der gebauten Wirklichkeit abgeschaut, die sie zugleich abstrahieren und idealisieren. Ihre Wirkung erzielen sie nicht durch Darstellung einer fiktiven Zukunft, sondern durch Bestätigung und Zuspitzung des Gegenwärtigen. Sie faszinieren, indem sie uns bekannt erscheinen. Sie irritieren, weil sie uns eine Wirklichkeit vorspielen, die so nicht ist.

Die architekturgalerie am weißenhof e. V. freut sich, dieses Wechselspiel zwischen Faszination und Irritation – zur Vermittlung von Architektur und als Anregung zum reflektierten Umgang mit unserer gebauten Umwelt – mit der Ausstellung märklinMODERNE zusammen mit der Schau im Deutschen Architekturmuseum (DAM) präsentieren zu können.

The architekturgalerie am weißenhof e. V., which has shown 175 exhibitions since it was founded in 1982 in Stuttgart, sees its task as the presentation of architecture in all media, including models.

Models of constructed, planned, or fictional architecture have been part of the history of architecture since ancient times. They were intended to give clients an idea of the building and also served as templates for further construction. Since the 15th century, models have become the norm for larger construction projects, fulfilling the functions of representative display objects and extended proportional planning instruments. Since then, they have also been accompanied by the criticism that they are not used to depict reality, but rather to deceive the observer.

The models in the exhibition märklinMODERNE must be assessed differently than "normal" architecture models. They copy built reality, simultaneously abstracting and idealizing it. Their impact stems not from the depiction of a fictional future, but rather from the confirmation and intensification of the present day. They are fascinating because they seem familiar. At the same time, they are irksome, because they simulate a reality which does not exist.

The architekturgalerie am weißenhof e. V. is pleased to be able to present this interplay between fascination and irritation—to convey architecture and as an impulse for a considered treatment of our built environment—with the märklinMODERNE exhibition together with the display at the German Architecture Museum (DAM).

Grußwort

Greeting

Architektur gestaltet unser Umfeld, formt die Räume, in denen wir leben und prägt manchmal auch unsere Kindheitserinnerungen mit einem Miniaturabbild unserer Welt: der Modelleisenbahn im Hobbykeller. Aber war die Modelleisenbahn nicht auch immer der Versuch, sich ein Wunschabbild für den utopischen „Originalzustand" unserer Städte und Landschaften in der Zeit irgendwann vor dem Zweiten Weltkrieg zu schaffen? Hat die Architektur der Nachkriegszeit überhaupt Einzug gehalten in die Häuschen-Bausätze der Modelleisenbahn?

Sie hat! Und die Ausstellung märklin-MODERNE sowie der Katalog zeichnen in beeindruckender Weise diesen Weg in die Alltags- und gleichzeitig auch die Wunschwelt der Modelleisenbahn nach. Sie leistet damit einen wichtigen Beitrag zur Rezeptionsgeschichte der Architektur der Zeit nach 1945.
Die Wüstenrot Stiftung hat mit Freude dazu beigetragen, dass das Projekt von moderneREGIONAL Wirklichkeit werden konnte. Nicht zuletzt, weil damit ein weiterer Schritt in Richtung allgemeiner Wertschätzung für die oft ungeliebte und in ihrem Wert oft noch unterschätzte „Nachkriegsmoderne" gegangen wird.

Architecture shapes our environment, forms the spaces in which we live, and also sometimes leaves its mark on our childhood memories with a miniature portrayal of our world: the model train set in the hobby room. But has the model railway not always also been an attempt to create an ideal portrayal of the utopian „original state" of our cities and landscapes from a time before the Second World War? Did the architecture of the post-war period find its way into the building assembly kits of the model railways at all?

It did! And the exhibition märklin-MODERNE and its catalog impressively portray the path of post-war architecture into the everyday and at the same time ideal world of model railways. It thus makes an important contribution to the history of the reception of post-1945 architecture. The Wüstenrot Stiftung was pleased to contribute to the successful realization of this project by moderne-REGIONAL. Not least because this project takes a further step towards improving the general regard for the often unpopular and underappreciated „post-war modernism."

BEITRÄGE UND GESPRÄCHE

ARTICLES AND INTERVIEWS

Moderne auf der Modellbahnplatte
Modernism on the model railway board

DANIEL BARTETZKO

MINIATURBAUTEN ZWISCHEN INDIVIDUALITÄT UND GROSSSERIE

MINIATURES BETWEEN INDIVIDUALITY AND LARGE-SCALE PRODUCTION

Im Jahr 1935 präsentierte die Firma Trix die 00-Eisenbahn im Maßstab 1:90. Bald folgten fast alle Hersteller dieser Größe, die 1950 noch von Doppelnull in Halbnull (H0/1:87) geändert wurde. In ihrer Anfangszeit blieb die sogenannte „Tisch-Bahn" ein Privileg der Gutbetuchten. Hermann Göring hortete in seinem Landsitz Carinhall nicht nur Raubkunst, sondern auch mehrere Modelleisenbahnen. Doch dieses Spielzeug ist ideologiefrei: Was sich auf der Modellplatte tut, entscheidet alleine ihr Erbauer. Hier darf zwischen vielgleisigen Schnellzugstrecken die Sinfonie einer Großstadt erklingen oder eine Bimmelbahn in ein Bergdorf-Idyll schnaufen. Während in den 1950er bis 1970er Jahren rastlos am Wirtschaftswunder gearbeitet wurde, sich die politische und gesellschaftliche Entwicklung immer weiter beschleunigte, versprach der Mikrokosmos Modellbahn Ruhe und Rückzug. Und bot gleichwohl jedes

In 1935, the company Trix presented the 00 train, on a scale of 1:90. Almost all manufacturers soon followed this scale, which was extended further from double zero to an H0 scale (1:87) in 1950. At the beginning, the so-called "table railway" remained a privilege for the wealthy. At his country estate Carinhall, Hermann Göring hoarded not only stolen art, but also several model train sets. However, this toy is free of ideologies; the model builder alone is responsible for what happens on the model board. Anything is possible, from multiple-track express train lines that shape the symphony of the big city to sightseeing coaches that puff through mountain village idylls. Between the 1950s and the 1970s, the Federal Republic worked tirelessly on the economic wonder; political and social development accelerated constantly. In this context, the microcosm of the model railway offered peace and withdrawal and,

Hermann Göring zeigt den Geburtstagsgästen auf seinem Anwesen Carinhall die Modellbahnanlage, 1943
Hermann Göring shows birthday guests the model train set at his Carinhall estate, 1943

Jahr genug Neuheiten, um auch Fortschrittsfreunde zu begeistern – Kinder sowieso. Dass der Nachwuchs stets mit Vätern und Großvätern um die Macht am Trafo konkurrieren musste, war im Sinne der Erfinder: Man hat das Spiel mit der kleinen Eisenbahn spätestens seit den frühen 1960ern als Hobby für die ganze Familie vermarktet – und sich damit generationsübergreifende Absatzmöglichkeiten gesichert.

at the same time novelties each year to also excite fans of progress—and children in any case. Admittedly, the constant competition between the younger generation and their fathers and grandfathers for control of the transformer was the creators' intent. Playing with miniature trains was marketed as a hobby for the whole family from the 1960s onward at the latest, thus ensuring cross-generational sales opportunities.

FLIEGENDE DÄCHER UND SCHLICHTE KUBEN

Während die Modellbahnproduzenten auf eine begrenzte Anzahl von Vorbildern zurückgreifen mussten, konnten die Häuschenbauer aus dem unermesslichen Fundus der Architektur schöpfen. Natürlich wollten sie Geld verdienen. Doch dass neben wirtschaftlichem Streben Passion, sorgfältige Recherche, vielleicht gar unverwirklichte (Architekten-)Träume eine Rolle spielten, offenbart der Blick ins Detail. Die modernen Bausätze des Marktführers Faller kennzeichneten bunte Geländer, schräge Wandabschlüsse und immer wieder mittig gefaltete Flugdächer. Wer den Faller-Heimatort Gütenbach besucht, findet sie wieder in den Villen der Firmengründer, in der Faller-Fabrik, beim ebenfalls dort ansässigen Uhrenhersteller Hanhart. Der Faller-„Hausarchitekt" Leopold Messmer entwarf diese Gebäude im Maßstab 1:1, die Modellbauer schufen variierende Nachbildungen – als Bahnhöfe, Stellwerke oder Wohnhäuser. Beim Konkurrenten Kibri herrschten gradlinigere Vorstellungen: Schlicht und kubisch hatte dort die Moderne zu sein. Die strengen

Formen forderten bisweilen schon in 87-facher Verkleinerung Respekt ein. Das Bahnhofsensemble Neu-Ulm hatten die Böblinger ebenso miniaturisiert wie den Bahnhof Kehl. Bei Vollmer in Stuttgart gab es ab den frühen 1960ern eine Auswahl gelb geklinkerter Bahn-Systembauten, dazu diverse moderne, schmucklose Einfamilienhäuser, deren Vorbilder in den gutbetuchten Randbezirken der Stadt zu suchen sein dürften. Als Entwickler von Altstadthäusern reüssierte Vollmer erst ab den 1970ern.

DIE KUNST DES SCHUMMELNS

Vordergründig sind Modellbahnhäuser verwandt mit Architekturmodellen. Doch es gibt einen entscheidenden Unterschied: Auf einer Modellbahnplatte würden maßstäblich eingedampfte Großbauten alle Dimensionen sprengen. In der Regel sind die Miniaturen stilisiert; die Kunst der Auslassung und des Maßstabssprungs ist gefragt. Und die des Schummelns: Selbst wenn Modellhäuser realitätsnah wirken, sind sie doch befreit von Bauvorschriften, Nutzerfreundlichkeit und den Gesetzen der Statik. Ob Fallers Turmcafé bei voller Auslastung auf

FLOATING ROOFS AND SIMPLE CUBES

While the model train producers had only a limited number of real-life examples to model them on, the model building producers could draw on a vast pool of architecture. Naturally, they wanted to earn money. However, a close look at the details reveals that, in addition to economic aspirations, passion, careful research, and possibly even unrealized (architectural) dreams played a role. The modernist assembly kits of the market leader, Faller, were marked by colorful railings, slanted connecting walls, and, time and again, floating roofs folded in the middle. Those who choose to visit Gütenbach, the home of Faller, will see these elements in the company founders' villas, the Faller factory, and at the watchmaker Hanhart, who is also located there. The Faller "house architect," Leopold Messmer, designed these buildings on a scale of 1:1 and the model building producers created varying reproductions—as train stations, signal towers, or houses. The concepts at rival Kibri followed straighter lines: their modernism was simple and cubist. At times, the strict forms

demanded respect, even reduced by a factor of 87. Böblinger miniaturized the train station ensemble Neu-Ulm and the Kehl station. From the early 1960s onward, Vollmer in Stuttgart produced a selection of yellow brick train system buildings, including a variety of austere modernist single-family homes whose role models could be found in the wealthy suburbs of the city. Vollmer only began developing historic city center buildings in the 1970s.

THE ART OF CHEATING

Superficially, model railway buildings are related to architecture models. However, there is also a significant difference. On a model railway board, large buildings condensed true-to-scale would exceed all dimensions. As a rule, miniatures are stylized; omissions and jumps

Kubisch-modern präsentiert sich das stilisierte Neu-Ulm im Kibri-Katalog von 1964
Stylized Neu-Ulm has a cubist-modernist flair in the 1964 Kibri catalog

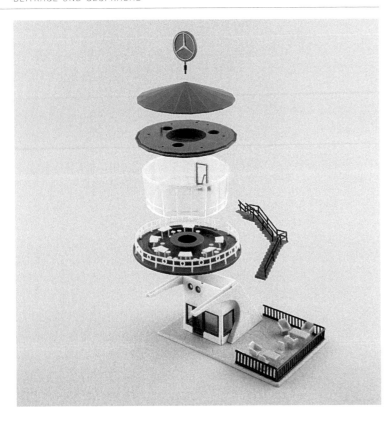

Befreit von den Zwängen der Statik:
der Faller-Bausatz „Auto-Rast", zer-
legt in seine Einzelteile
Freed from the confines of statics:
the Faller assembly kit "rest stop"
disassembled into its individual parts

in scale are required. And the art of cheating. Even though model buildings appear realistic, they are freed from building codes, user-friendliness, and the laws of static forces. Would the service station in Faller's lower café survive a full load on the floating roof? The Faller high-rise can only be entered through a shop; the GDR counterpart from Vero even adjusted the usual model railway scale between the ground floor and the upper floors from 1:87 to 1:160. The harmonious overall impression is what counts, without giving the model builder the feeling that overly crude details are being imposed on them.

INJECTION MOLDING AND SYSTEM CONSTRUCTION

Since the 1950s, the (West German) miniature houses have been produced using a plastic injection molding process. A collection of steel forms weighing tons is the treasure trove of every model producer. The form is cooled to a specific temperature, and then liquid plastic is injected under high pressure. After the model has hardened, the form is opened, allowing the finished ele-

ments of the injection-molded part to be released. To quote the children's program moderator Peter Lustig: "Sounds easy, but it isn't." The art of the tool maker is first to construct the mold so that the parts do not warp after the plastic is injected. Ultimately, the model producer has to pay attention to the cooling of the entire machine, the correct flow pressure, and the temperature. Seconds count when the molded parts come out of the machine and fall into a tempered box or water bath. Injection molding technology makes all sorts of small system parts possible—not just modernist ones. In plastic, half-timbered, historicized, Bauhaus, and avant-garde are all equally possible.

HORST SEEHOFER, ROD STEWART, AND NEIL YOUNG

The shrinking model railway scene is not as inactive as one might imagine. The pop-culturally-socialized intellectual who smirks because CSU politician Horst Seehofer has a model railway in his hobby room would be well advised to note that Rod Stewart and Neil Young also enjoy a part-time role as train conductors. This excessive bourgeoisie is as unexpected from

Faller verwahrt und nutzt in Gütenbach im Schwarzwald weiter die
Jahrzehnte zurückreichende Formen-
sammlung
In Gütenbach, Faller stores and uses
a collection of forms which spans
decades

dem Flugdach der darunterliegen-
den Tankstelle halten würde? Das
Faller-Hochhaus kann nur durch
den Eingang eines Ladengeschäfts
betreten werden, die DDR-Pendants
von Vero ändern vom Erdgeschoss
zu den oberen Etagen gar die
Modellbahn-Nenngröße von 1:87 in
1:160. Was zählt, ist der stimmige
Gesamteindruck, ohne dass sich ein
Bastler durch allzu krude Details auf
den Arm genommen fühlt.

SPRITZGUSS UND SYSTEM-BAUTEN

Seit den 1950er Jahren entstehen
die (westdeutschen) Mini-Häuser im
Kunststoffspritzguss-Verfahren. Eine
tonnenschwere Stahlformensamm-
lung ist die Schatzkammer jedes
Modellproduzenten: In die gezielt
gekühlte Form wird mit hohem Druck

flüssiger Kunststoff eingespritzt. Nach
dessen Aushärten fallen die fertigen
Elemente am sogenannten Spritzling
aus der aufgeklappten Form. Um den
Kinderfernseh-Moderator Peter Lustig

the two musicians as it is from club
owners Frederik and Gerrit Braun,
who run the Miniature Wonderland
in Hamburg. Faller is still the industry
leader; Kibri and Voller now belong

to Viessmann, a latecomer to this
segment, founded in 1988. "Art
in the age of its technical repro-
ducibility"—it is still happening on
the model board. However, in this

zu zitieren: „Klingt einfach, ist es aber nicht." Die Kunst des Werkzeugmachers ist es zunächst, die Gussform so zu konstruieren, dass sich die Bauteile nach dem Spritzen nicht verziehen. Der Modellbauer selbst muss schließlich die Kühlung der gesamten Maschine, den korrekten Fließdruck und die Temperatur im Auge behalten. Es zählen Sekunden, wenn das Werkstück ausgeworfen wird und in eine temperierte Box oder ein Wasserbad fällt. Die Spritzguss-Technologie ermöglicht lauter kleine Systembauten – nicht nur moderne. Ob Fachwerk, Historismus, Bauhaus oder Avantgarde: In Plastik sind alle gleich.

HORST SEEHOFER, ROD STEWART UND NEIL YOUNG

Die schrumpfende Modellbahnszene liegt nicht so brach, wie man meinen mag. Wer als popkulturell sozialisierter Intellektueller darüber lächelt, dass der CSU-Politiker Horst Seehofer eine Eisenbahn im Hobbykeller baut, dem sei gesagt, dass auch Rod Stewart und Neil Young als Teilzeit-Lokomotivführer wirken. Die Musiker sind übermäßiger Bürger-

lichkeit ebenso unverdächtig wie die ehemaligen Diskothekeninhaber Frederik und Gerrit Braun, die das Hamburger Miniatur Wunderland betreiben. Faller ist noch immer Marktführer, Kibri und Vollmer gehören heute der 1988 gegründeten Firma Viessmann, einem Späteinsteiger in diesem Segment. „Das Kunstwerk im Zeitalter seiner technischen Reproduzierbarkeit" – auf der Modellbahnplatte findet es noch immer statt. Doch hier verliert das Werk durch Vervielfältigung nicht seine Aura, wie Walter Benjamin 1936 in seinem Essay schrieb. Die Modelle erhalten sie erst durch die Reproduktion und dadurch, wie fähige oder mäßig begabte Bastlerhände die Teile zusammenfügen. Der süddeutsche Modellbauer Gerald Fuchs treibt es heute im wahren Wortsinn auf die Spitze, wenn er dutzende alte Stadthaus-Bausätze zu einem monumentalen Großbau kombiniert. Doch egal, wer wie was baut, die Erkenntnis ist: Gute Architektur kann durch keinen Kleberfleck beschädigt werden.

case the creation does not lose its aura through reproduction, as Walter Benjamin wrote in his 1936 essay. Quite the contrary: the models gain their aura through the reproduction itself and through their assembly by more or less skilled model builders. The southern German model builder Gerald Fuchs quite literally pushes this to the limits through his combination of dozens of single house assembly kits into a monumental large-format building. Regardless of who builds what and how, the message remains: good architecture cannot be spoiled by glue stains.

Gerald Fuchs errichtet wahrhaft
Großes aus dutzenden alter Stadt-
hausbausätze
Gerald Fuchs builds something truly
great from dozens of old assembly
kits

KARIN BERKEMANN

WERBEBILDER FÜR MODELLBAUER

ADVERTISING IMAGES FOR MODEL BUILDERS

Hektisch heute? Da hätten Sie erst einmal das Jahr 1961 erleben sollen! Gegen die „Hast" jener Tage bewarben die süddeutschen Modell-bau-Fabrikanten Hermann und Edwin Faller damals ihre Miniaturhäuser als „heilsames" Hobby. Der anspruchs-volle Kunde sollte sich beim lärm- und mühelosen Basteln entspannen. Die anspruchsvolle Kundin hinge-gen trat in den bunter werdenden Faller-Katalogen nur äußerst selten in Erscheinung. Und weil ja bekannt-lich nichts politischer ist als das angestrengt Unpolitische, schwang in den Werbebildern jener Jahre immer auch ein Stück Familien- und Weltbild mit: Während da draußen eine Mauer, zwei Blöcke und diverse interstellare Wettrennen hochgezo-gen wurden, war die Moderne auf der bundesdeutschen Modellbahn-platte eine betont harmonische.

If you think life is hectic today, you should have seen 1961! Southern German model producers Hermann and Edwin Faller marketed their miniature buildings as a "salutary" hobby to counter the "haste" charac-teristic of the time. Demanding (male) consumers should be able to relax through noiseless and effortless handicrafts. The demanding female consumer, on the other hand, only appeared extremely infrequently in the ever-more-colorful Faller cata-logs. And because it is well-known that nothing is more political than attempted a-politicalness, the adver-tising images of that era also always reflected the dominant family and world view. While in the real world the Berlin Wall was being erected, two blocs were being formed, and a variety of interstellar races were underway, modernism on the West German model railway board was emphatically harmonious.

Das Modell der Falzarego-Kapelle
liegt im Faller-Katalog 1961 in gut
manikürten Händen
A model of the Falzarego chapel
in the Faller catalog from 1961 is
presented by well-manicured hands

THE WORLD BECOMES COLORFUL

The miniature train stations and buildings of the first years after the Second World War were made of sheet metal, wood, and cardboard and were black and white, at least in the catalogs of companies such as Faller, Kibri, and Vollmer. In the early, still modest brochures, only the title pages had single-color backgrounds or contained text which was highlighted with color. Black and white photographs, which were very similar to graphics when printed, were supplemented by various types of explanatory text. People did not play a significant role in the images. In a rare instance from 1956, Kibri elevated a boy, who beamingly completes a train station assembly kit, to a cipher. The stylistic devices of the train station and the graphic itself refer more to the first half of the 20th century than the second.

Neuheiten 1956

Kibri

Für den Kibri-Katalog 1956 bastelt der Bub freudig eine der beworbenen Neuheiten
A boy happily tinkers with one of the novelties advertised in the 1956 Kibri catalog

sprinkled throughout. The new plastic models constituted their own cosmos, and were grouped to make villages and cities complete with miniature people. The highest degree of Hollywood drama was achieved when a steam engine appeared to drive out of the pages towards the reader. And when shaded or dotted areas were connected with text, a foreshadowing of Roy Lichtenstein nearly drove through the Black Forest. Indeed, Faller and Kibri maintained an American clientele from the era of occupation which they fostered through English-language catalogs.

USER MANUAL OR SEX APPEAL?

From 1957 onward, Faller responded to the need for an all-round user manual. The "Faller Model Building Mag-

DIE WELT WIRD BUNT

Die Miniaturbahnhöfe und -häuser der ersten Nachkriegsjahre waren aus Blech, Holz und Pappe. Und schwarz-weiß, zumindest in den Katalogen von Firmen wie Faller, Kibri und Vollmer. Hier wurden für die frühen, noch überschaubaren

Broschüren höchstens die Titelblätter in einer Farbe hinterlegt oder einzelne Schriftzüge farbig hervorgehoben. Schwarz-Weiß-Fotografien, die im Druck einer Grafik sehr nahe kamen, ergänzte man um allerlei erklärenden Text. Menschen spielten hier im Bild keine prägende Rolle. In einem der seltenen Fälle erhob

While the black outlines do not show it, today's observer fills in the image with blonde hair and blue eyes. Color was introduced into the Faller catalog in the middle of the 1950s. Model landscapes glowed from the title pages, while in the interior, individual photos were displayed in color and colorful graphics were

Kibri 1956 einen Jungen, der gerade strahlend einen Bahnhof-Bausatz vollendet, zur Chiffre. Die Stilmittel des Bahnhofs wie der Grafik verweisen eher in die erste, als in die zweite Hälfte des 20. Jahrhunderts. Ohne dass es die schwarzen Linien zeigen würden, vervollständigt der heutige Betrachter das Motiv um blondes Haar und blaue Augen.

Die Mehrfarbigkeit war Mitte der 1950er Jahre schon in die Faller-Kataloge eingezogen. Auf den Titelblättern leuchteten Modelllandschaften, im Innenteil wurden einzelne Fotos koloriert und zwischendurch farbige Grafiken eingestreut. Aus den neuen Plastik-Modellen war ein eigener Kosmos gewachsen, der mit Miniaturmenschen zu Dörfern und Städten gruppiert wurde. Das Höchstmaß an Hollywood war erreicht, wenn eine Dampflok auf den Leser zuzufahren schien. Und wenn schraffierte oder punktierte Flächen mit Schrift verbunden wurden, zog fast schon eine Vorahnung von Roy Lichtenstein durch den Schwarzwald. Hatten sich Faller und Kibri doch noch aus Besatzungszeiten einen amerikanischen Kundenkreis bewahrt und mit englischsprachigen Prospekten ausgebaut.

LEBENSHILFE ODER SEX-APPEAL?

Ab 1957 entsprach Faller dem Bedürfnis nach einer allumfassenden Lebenshilfe: Das „Faller Modellbau Magazin" (ab 1977: „Welt der Modellbahn") erschien mit einem Farbcover, das Innenleben der Hefte blieb schwarz-weiß. Fotos wurden um technische Detailzeichnungen

azine" (from 1977 onward: "World of Model Trains") was published with a full-color cover; the interior remained black and white. Photos were supplemented with technical detail drawings, as clarity was foremost. In this case, however, a real rarity in comparison to the catalogs, model builders could sometimes be observed going about their hobby. The miniature and real words were

Im Faller-Katalog 1961 präsentiert der Junge dem Mädchen stolz sein Hochhausmodell
A boy proudly presents a girl his high-rise model in the Faller catalog from 1961

allowed to meet briefly. The consumer handouts "1000 possibilities with Vollmer parts" followed a similar method. These were published more infrequently, but were therefore more detailed and with more color. For East German fans of TT scale rails, the magazine "Model Train Practice," which had a look similar to the first Faller magazines, was published in the 1960s and 1970s.

As a family business, Faller specifically produced their models for families. Around 1960, the catalogs regularly featured color photos of parents and children happily constructing models together. The female participants decorated the landscape while the male participants controlled the technical aspects. Equal opportunity happened in small but continuous steps. In 1961, a boy and a girl were presented on an equal footing in an advertising image (the Faller brothers

MODELLBAHN ZUBEHÖR Spur H0

Kibri seit 1895

Im Katalog von 1959 findet Kibri in seinen Grafiken zu kunstvoller Abstraktion
In 1959, Kibri's catalog graphics began to be artistic abstractions

bereichert – Hauptsache, deutlich. Doch, eine echte Seltenheit im Vergleich zu den Katalogen, hier waren gelegentlich echte Bastler bei ihrem Hobby zu sehen, hier durften sich Miniatur- und Alltagswelt kurz berühren. Einen ähnlichen Ansatz verfolgten

die Kundenhandreichungen „1000 Möglichkeiten mit Vollmer-Teilen", Diese erschienen seltener, dafür waren sie aufwendiger und farbiger ausgestaltet. Für den ostdeutschen Spur-TT-Fan gab es in den 1960er und 1970er Jahren, in ihrem Look

had only daughters). The core message was however the same: the boy builds—in this case the Faller highrise—and the girl admires him for it. The catalog attempted glamor only once, in the catalog from the same year. There, a blonde in a figure-hug-

ging outfit tenderly presents a model of the Falzarego chapel. While a male observer might complain that the scale of the H0 assembly kit is not correct, the female observer is already googling where the woman's outfit can be bought today.

den ersten Faller-Magazinen nicht unähnlich, die Zeitschrift „Modellbahn Praxis".

Als Familienunternehmen produzierte Faller ausdrücklich für Familien. Wenn auf den nunmehr gerne freigestellten Farbfotos um 1960 Eltern und Kinder traulich vereint Modelle bauten, dekorierte die weibliche Seite die Landschaft, während der männliche Part die Technik kontrollierte. Gleichberechtigung vollzog sich in kleinen, aber feinen Schritten: 1961 begegneten sich Junge und Mädchen bei einer der Werbegrafiken auf Augenhöhe (immerhin hatten die Faller-Brüder ausschließlich Töchter). Im Kern blieb es aber dabei: Der Bub baute – in diesem Fall das Faller-Hochhaus – und das Mädel bewunderte ihn dafür. Nur einmal setzte man im Katalog desselben Jahres auf Glamour: Da präsentierte eine figurnah bekleidete Blondine zärtlich ein Modell der Falzarego-Kapelle. Rückblickend mag der Betrachter nörgeln, dass der Maßstab des H0-Bausatzes verfälscht wird, während die Betrachterin schon längst googelt, wo es das Outfit der Werbeträgerin heute wieder zu kaufen gibt.

DAS BILD MACHT DIE WIRKLICHKEIT

Während Kibri um 1960 noch formidable Grafiken im Mondrian-Stil schuf, schwenkte die Firma um 1965 zu einem konsequenten Fotorealismus – ein Trend, dem große Mitbewerber wie Vollmer und kleinere Hersteller wie VauPe bald folgten. Die Faller-Kataloge fanden erst spät auf diesen Weg, stattdessen wurde die gewohnt wohlgeordnete Modellbauwelt zunächst vor psychedelisch gefärbten Hintergründen präsentiert. Auch der Anbieter OWO zeigte die DDR in miniature architektonisch und grafisch durchaus modern: große Farbflächen und ein gerüttelt Maß Abstraktion. Der ostdeutsche Traditionsbetrieb Auhagen hingegen, dessen Häuschen damals vor allem einer historisierenden Erzgebirgs-Idylle verpflichtet waren, vollzog um 1970 fast nahtlos den Sprung vom Schwarz-Weiß- zum durchgängigen Farbfoto. Aber die Richtung war klar: Je näher das Modellbild der – zugegebenermaßen sehr aufgeräumten – gebauten Wirklichkeit kam, desto besser für den Verkauf.

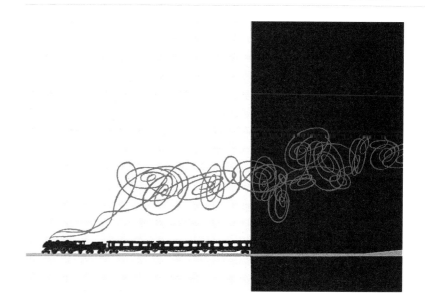

THE IMAGE MAKES REALITY

Around 1960, Kibri was producing formidable Mondrian-style graphics; however, around 1965, the company shifted to consistent photo-realism —a trend which both their major competitors like Vollmer and smaller producers such as VauPe soon followed. The Faller catalog followed this trend somewhat later; instead, the usual, well-ordered world of model buildings was presented at first on psychedelic color backgrounds. The producer OWO displayed the GDR in miniature in an architecturally and graphically modern way: large color fields and a high degree of abstraction. The East German traditional producer Auhagen on the other hand, whose buildings were committed above all to a historicizing Ore Mountains idyll, completed a nearly seamless jump from black and white images to all color photos around 1970. But the direction was clear:

Zwei Hochhäuser im Werbebild: das westdeutsche Faller-Modell im Jahr 1971 und das ostdeutsche Vero-Modell in den 1970er Jahren
Two high-rises in advertising: the West German Faller model from 1971 and the East German Vero model from the 1970s

Oft verschwamm die Grenze zwischen Foto und Realität, zwischen Vorbild und Abbild. Nicht zufällig veröffentlichte Faller wiederholt den Hochhaus-Bausatz zusammen mit Fotos des formal sehr ähnlichen Gütenbacher Firmensitzes. Um 1970 heftete man dann noch den Faller-Schriftzug an die Miniaturfassade. Ähnlich ging der ostdeutsche Mitbewerber Vero ans Werk, als er sein Modellhochhaus in eine Aufnahme der Messestadt Leipzig montierte. Damit wurden beide Hochhäuser zu Bedeutungsträgern stilisiert: Während das Faller-Hochhaus zum eigenen kapitalistischen Werbezeichen geriet, vertrat das Vero-Modell sinnfällig das sozialistische Zukunftsversprechen. Auch im Privaten wurden die Neuheitenkataloge und Weihnachtsbeilagen zu Sehnsuchtsbildern. Und so mancher Architekt räumt heute in fortgeschrittener Bierlaune ein, dass er sich für sein Wohnhaus beim ein oder anderen Detail des Modells „Villa im Tessin" bedient hat.

PARTY IM HOBBYKELLER (ODER UMGEKEHRT)

Die Bausätze der Nachkriegsjahrzehnte wurden von Männern entworfen, von Frauen und Kindern in Heimarbeit verpackt und zuletzt vom Vater an den Sohne verschenkt – nur der letzte Teil dieser Kette tauchte um 1960 (wenn überhaupt) in den Werbebildern auf. In den Faller-Katalogfotos wurde der menschliche Part zunehmend auf Miniaturfigürchen der Firma Preiser beschränkt, nichts sollte die im Hobbykeller herbeigebastelte Ordnung stören. Der belebte Partyspaß war für andere Faller-Produkte reserviert: Adrette Pärchen trafen sich im flauschigen Wohnzimmer zum Rennen auf der Modellautobahn „ams", während die Kinder mit HITtrain und HITcar bespaßt wurden. Und hier durften – ungeheuerlich – sichtbar auch die Frauen ans Steuer.

the closer that the model image came to the—albeit very tidy—built reality, the better it sold.

The border between photos and reality, between the ideal and its copy, was often blurred. It was no coincidence that Faller repeatedly published their high-rise assembly kit together with photos of their formally very similar company headquarters in Gütenbach. Around 1970, the miniature facade was even outfitted with the Faller sign. The East German competitor Vero took a similar tack, positioning its model high-rise in front of a photo of the congress city Leipzig. In this way, both high-rises were stylized into carriers of meaning: while the Faller high rise became a capitalist advertisement for the company, the Vero model obviously represented the socialist promise of the future. In private, the catalogs of new releases and the Christmas special editions became objects of longing as well. And it is not unheard of for architects today to admit after a few drinks that they adopted details from the model "Villa in Ticino" for their own house.

PARTY IN THE HOBBY ROOM (OR THE OTHER WAY AROUND)

The assembly kits of the post-war decades were designed by men, packed by women and children working from home, and then gifted from father to son. Around 1960, only the last part of this chain (if at all) appeared in the advertising images. In the photos in the Faller catalog, the appearance of people was increasingly limited to miniature figures from the Preiser company; nothing should disturb the order in the hobby room. Lively fun at parties was reserved for other Faller products: well-dressed couples met in the living room to race model cars on the "ams" track, while children amused themselves with the HITtrain and HITcar. And here—unbelievably—women were visibly also allowed a turn behind the wheel.

„Manchmal war auch ein bisschen Spiel dabei"
"Sometimes there was playfulness in the process"

DER ARCHITEKT LEOPOLD MESSMER
ÜBER LIEBLINGSPROJEKTE
ZWISCHEN VILLA UND HOCHHAUS

ARCHITECT LEOPOLD MESSMER
ABOUT HIS FAVORITE PROJECTS
FROM VILLAS TO HIGH-RISES

Er wohnt im Schwarzwald, in einem Hochhaus: Wir besuchen den Architekten Leopold Messmer (*1928) zu Hause in Villingen. Seine Wohnung liegt direkt unterm Dach. Fast ist man versucht, von einem Penthouse zu sprechen, wenn das nicht einen Hauch zu mondän klänge. „Modern sollte es schon sein, aber auch ein bisschen nach Heimat aussehen", so beschreibt Messmer die Wünsche seiner Auftraggeber der 1950er und 1960er Jahre. Doch Stil hat sein heutiges Domizil sicher, immerhin führt der Fahrstuhl direkt bis in die Wohnung. Und der weite Rundumblick, der ist unbezahlbar. Ganz in der Nähe liegt der Firmensitz von Faller. In Gütenbach, einem Ort, den Messmer vom selbstbewussten Hochhaus bis zur futuristischen Villa in die Moderne katapultiert hat. Was das alles mit dem Modellbau zu tun hat, erzählt er im Gespräch mit Daniel Bartetzko und Karin Berkemann:

He lives in a high-rise in the Black Forest. We visited architect Leopold Messmer (*1928) at his home in Villingen. His apartment is on the top floor, under the roof. One is almost tempted to describe it as a penthouse, if that didn't sound just a bit too fashionable. "It should be modern, but also have a touch of home"; that's how Messmer described what his employer wanted in the 1950s and 60s. His current home definitely has style; the elevator opens directly into his apartment. And the panoramic view is priceless. The Faller company headquarters are located nearby in Gütenbach, a town which Messmer catapulted into modernism with confident high-rises and futuristic villas. In a conversation with Daniel Bartetzko and Karin Berkemann, he explains what all that has to do with models.

Daniel Bartetzko [DB]
Mr. Messmer, the brothers Edwin and Hermann Faller founded their

Der Faller-„Hausarchitekt" Leopold Messmer im Gespräch mit Daniel Bartetzko
Faller "house architect" Leopold Messmer speaks with Daniel Bartetzko

Daniel Bartetzko [DB] *Herr Messmer, die Brüder Edwin und Hermann Faller begründeten nach dem Krieg ihre Modellbaufirma. Wie haben Sie die beiden erlebt?*

Leopold Messmer [LM] Der Hermann war der Tuftler, er hatte das ganze Geschäft aufgebaut. Der Edwin war der Kaufmann, er hat das Finanzielle besorgt. Er hat sehr gut gemalt, da war er wirklich ein Künstler. Beide waren für mich viel mehr als Bauherren. Das war eine Freundschaft, die wir zusammen hatten.

DB *Sie waren über Jahrzehnte der „Hausarchitekt" der Fallers. Wann begann die Zusammenarbeit?*

LM Die Firma Faller ist 1954/55 im Zuge ihrer Baumaßnahmen an mich herangetreten. Die haben ja sehr viel gebaut in Gütenbach, zum Beispiel die Hochhäuser und die Villen. Da war ich als Architekt überall mit involviert.

Karin Berkemann [KB] *Nur bei den „großen" Bauten?*

LM Nein, parallel dazu wurde ich immer wieder bei den Modellbauten eingeschaltet. Ich habe dabei beraten und manchmal auch Pläne gemacht. Bei den Modellen war ich sicher zu 70, 80 Prozent beteiligt.

KB *Nehmen wir eines der frühesten wirklich modernen Faller-Modelle, das Hochhaus, das 1958 auf den Markt kam. Gab es dafür ein reales Vorbild?*

LM Das Hochhausmodell ist entstanden durch das große Faller-Hochhaus in Gütenbach, das ich entworfen habe. Das zu gestalten, war natürlich in dem engen Tal nicht einfach. Zu Beginn hatte der Bau vier Stockwerke. Dann brauchte man mehr Platz und es kam während des Baus noch ein Stock dazu und noch ein Stock. Das Gütenbacher Hochhaus war das Vorbild für das Modell, beide entstanden parallel. Dieser Bau war mir am sympathischsten, denn ich habe seitdem kein Hochhaus in diesem Sinn mehr gebaut.

DB *Das Vorbild für den Faller-Bausatz „Villa im Tessin" aus dem Jahr*

model company after the Second World War. What was your impression of them?

Leopold Messmer [LM] Hermann was the tinkerer. He was the one who built up the company. Edwin was the businessman—he was in charge of the finances. He painted very well; he was really an artist in that regard. The two of them were much more than clients to me. We were friends.

DB *You were the Faller "house architect" for decades. When did the cooperation begin?*

LM The Faller company came to me in 1954/55 over the course of their various construction projects. They built a lot in Gütenbach, for example the high-rises and the villas. I was the architect for the vast majority of these projects.

Karin Berkemann [KB] *Just the "full-scale" buildings?*

LM No, parallel to these projects, I was repeatedly involved in the models. I gave them advice and sometimes I even drew up plans. I was involved in the models up to 70, 80 percent.

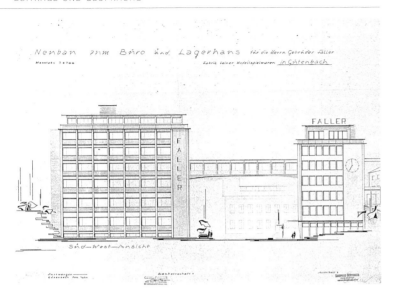

1961 stand tatsächlich im Tessin, in Ambrì in der Nähe vom Gotthardtunnel: ein mondänes Wohnhaus, das 1958 von Aldo und Alberto Guscetti errichtet wurde. Wie haben die Faller-Brüder diesen Bau kennengelernt?

LM Wenn der Hermann durch das Tessin fuhr, fuhr er immer an diesem Gebäude vorbei. Und da hat er gesagt: „So eins will ich einmal haben!" Das war die Villa im Tessin, das Projekt, das mir am liebsten war. Etwas, das nicht alltäglich ist.

Leopold Messmer, hier sein Plan aus dem Dezember 1960, erweiterte die Faller-Werke in Gütenbach im Schwarzwald
Leopold Messmer—here is his plan from December 1960—expanded the Faller factory in Gütenbach in the Black Forest

KB Let's take the earliest really modernist Faller model, the high-rise which was released in 1958. Was it based on a real building?

LM The high-rise model emerged as a result of the large Faller high-rise in Gütenbach which I designed. It wasn't easy to design it in the narrow valley there. In the beginning, the building had four floors. Then they needed more space; during construction, first one additional floor was added, and then a second one. The model was based on the high-rise in Gütenbach; the two were created at the same time. This is one of my favorite buildings, since I haven't built a high-rise like that since then.

DB The Faller assembly kit "Villa in Ticino" from 1961 was actually based on a building in Ticino, in Ambrì, near the Gotthard Tunnel; a fashionable, single-family home which was built in 1958 by Aldo and Alberto Guscetti. How did the Faller brothers learn about this building?

LM When Hermann drove through Ticino, he always drove by this building. And he said: "One day, I want one like that!" That was the Villa in Ticino, my favorite project of all. Something which wasn't just run-of-the-mill.

KB Where did you study architecture?

LM I didn't have a high school diploma; I studied carpentry. My father had a carpentry business. Then I studied architecture in Karlsruhe, but not at the TH. I studied at the Staatstechnikum. I completed a one-year internship with Egon Eiermann. During that period, the Kaiser Willhelm memorial church in Berlin was renovated and the two modernist buildings, "lipstick and powder case," were constructed.

KB And later? Where did you gather your architectural inspiration?

LM Good architecture was rare back then. We went to visit buildings which interested us in Karlsruhe and Stuttgart together with Hermann Faller. The "Rest stop" model for example was based on a building that the Fallers saw on a family outing in Freiburg.

KB In the meantime, you had founded your own office in Furtwangen. Is this wooden figure a present from your employees for the 40th anniversary of that event?

LM Yes, I had the largest architecture office in the area; at one point, we had twelve to fifteen employees, especially in industrial construction.

Nach einem Vorbild im Tessin errichtete Leopold Messmer in Gütenbach eine Villa
Leopold Messmer built a villa in Gütenbach based on a single-family home in Ticino

KB Wo haben Sie Architektur studiert?

LM Ich hatte kein Abitur und habe zuerst Zimmermann gelernt – mein Vater hatte ein Zimmergeschäft. Dann habe ich in Karlsruhe Architektur studiert, aber nicht an der TH, sondern am Staatstechnikum. Bei Egon Eiermann war ich ein Jahr als Praktikant tätig. In jener Zeit wurde in Berlin die Kaiser-Wilhelm-Gedächtnis-Kirche saniert und die beiden modernen Zubauten „Lippenstift und Puderdose" entstanden.

KB Wo haben Sie sich später Ihre architektonischen Anregungen geholt?

LM Gute Architektur war damals rar. Speziell mit dem Hermann Faller haben wir uns immer wieder entsprechende Objekte angeschaut, die uns interessiert haben: in Karlsruhe und in Stuttgart. Das Vorbild für das

Modell „Auto-Rast" hatten die Fallers zum Beispiel bei einem Familienausflug in Freiburg gesehen.

KB Sie hatten sich inzwischen in Furtwangen selbstständig gemacht. Diese Holzfigur ist ein Geschenk Ihrer Mitarbeiter zum 40-jährigen Bürojubiläum?

LM Ja, ich hatte im Kreis Jahrzehnte das größte Architekturbüro, da waren zeitweilig zwölf bis fünfzehn Leute beschäftigt, speziell im Industriebau. Den ersten Nagel bei Faller, den habe ich in die Wand geschlagen. Und das macht jetzt unser Sohn, der führt das Architekturbüro fort. Meine Frau war auch voll im Büro tätig und seit vier, fünf Wochen weiß ich, dass mein Enkel weitergeht. Er hat jetzt das Abitur hinter sich und studiert in Konstanz Architektur.

DB Dann schauen Sie heute mit Freude auf Ihre Arbeit zurück?

LM Ich bin gut zufrieden. Der ganze Beruf hat mir immer Spaß gemacht.

DB Und was hat Sie speziell an den Modellbauten gereizt?

LM Ich bin selbst gar kein Modellbahner. Das Mitplanen an den Modellen war praktisch eine Sache, die man im wahren Baubetrieb mitgemacht hat – und manchmal war auch ein bisschen Spiel dabei.

I was the one who hammered the first nail in the first wall at Faller's. Now our son has taken over; he's now in charge of the architecture office. My wife also worked in the office. And four or five weeks ago I learned that my grandson is going to continue the family business. He just got his high school diploma and is studying architecture in Constance.

DB Then you look back on your work today with satisfaction?

LM Yes, I am very satisfied. The whole profession was always very enjoyable for me.

DB And what was it that you liked about models in particular?

LM I myself am not a model railway enthusiast. I planned the models as part of the construction process. But sometimes there was playfulness in the process.

Architekturmodelle und Modellbahnhäuschen
Architectural models and model railway houses

OLIVER ELSER

WAS SIE TRENNT UND VERBINDET

WHAT CONNECTS AND SEPARATES THEM

Der Modelleisenbahner hat mit allerhand Widrigkeiten zu kämpfen. Die Verkleinerung der realen Welt auf den gängigen Maßstab 1:87, auch H0 oder „Halbnull" genannt, bringt oft faszinierende, häufig aber auch frustrierende Ergebnisse hervor. Man kann sich für einige hundert Euro eine Lokomotive kaufen, bei der selbst feinste Beschriftungen, Schrauben oder Radspeichen mit höchster Präzision wiedergegeben sind. Aber wehe dem, der an dieses Wunderwerk der Feinmechanik noch ein paar Wagen anspannen will. Ein normaler Reisezugwaggon wäre, maßstäblich korrekt dargestellt, für die normale private Modellbahnplatte viel zu lang. Wer hat schon einen Bahnsteig von 2,30 Metern Länge, um einen ICE mit acht Wagen unterzubringen, der im Original gut 200 Meter lang ist? Auch die Kurven sind oft viel zu eng. Dieses Missverhältnis zwischen Anspruch und Möglichkeiten wiederholt sich bei

Model railway builders have a whole range of adversities to deal with. The miniaturization of the real world to the usual scale of 1:87, also known as H0, produces often fascinating, but also frequently frustrating, results. For a few hundred euros, one can buy a locomotive on which the finest lettering, screws, and spokes are reproduced with the highest precision. But there's no chance of attaching a few cars to this wonder of precision engineering. A normal passenger train carriage reproduced true-to-scale would be entirely too long for the normal private model railway board. Who has a train platform 2.3 meters long to fit an ICE with eight cars, which is more than 200 meters long in real life? The curves are also often much too tight. This disparity between aspiration and ability is repeated in the architecture. Much like the passenger carriages, most of the models of buildings are much too small. They have to be—otherwise

Die heimische Modellbahnplatte setzt
– hier im Faller-Magazin im Oktober
1968 – einer maßstabsgetreuen
Wiedergabe von Bahnen und Bauten
enge Grenzen
The domestic model railway board—
here in the Faller magazine in
October 1968—tight limitations on a
true-to-scale reproduction of trains
and buildings

der Architektur. Die meisten Modelle von Bauwerken sind, ebenso wie die Waggons, eigentlich viel zu klein geraten. Sie müssen es sein, weil sie sonst die Dimension der heimischen Eisenbahnanlage sprengen und dem Modellbahner seine beschränkten Mittel schmerzlich in Erinnerung bringen würden. Der Maßstab 1:87 gilt allenfalls für die Höhe, so gut wie nie aber für die Länge und Tiefe eines Gebäudes. Die meisten Einfamilienhäuser aus dem Modellbahnbedarf entsprechen eigentlich geräumigen Gartenlauben, weil sich kaum mehr als ein einziges Zimmer pro Geschoss darin unterbringen ließe, würde man den behaupteten Maßstab wirklich ernst nehmen.

ADRETT UND SAUBER GEKÄRCHERT

Ob ein Modell maßstäblich korrekt ist oder wie die überwiegende Zahl der Modellbahnhäuser einfach zu knubbelig wirkt und daher trotz aller feinen Detaillierung letztlich wie ein Spielzeug aussieht, das fällt dem Laien sicher nicht auf. Architekten aber schauen mit Verachtung auf die Welt der Faller-Häuser. Auch die sterile bis grelle Farbigkeit und der speckige Glanz der durchgefärbten Plastikbauteile fallen unangenehm auf. Es ist bezeichnend, dass sie nicht in einem neutralen Grau angeboten werden wie etwa die ebenfalls beliebten Modelle von Schiffen, Flugzeugen oder, tja, oft auch Panzern. Patina und Schmutz, abgeplatzter Lack und realistisch nachgeahmte Ölflecken sind in diesem Modellbau-Genre die Kennzeichen wahrer Meisterschaft. Das sind jedoch Themen, mit denen sich der normale H0er offensichtlich nicht beschäftigen will. Sonst wären in den Bausätzen die Dächer nicht ziegelrot, die Fensterrahmen weiß und das Fachwerk so ekelhaft braun, dass man fast schon wieder einen perfiden höheren Sinn darin vermuten könnte. Das zusammengeklebte Ergebnis kommt dann so clean und neu daher, wie eine deutsche Kleinstadt sich eben auch in der Realität präsentiert. Da aber auszuschließen ist, dass die Modellbahnbausätze eigentlich eine Kritik am deutschen Sauberkeits- und Sanierungswahn befördern sollen, muss man weiterhin davon ausgehen, dass der 1:87-Bastler einfach keine Lust hat, sich mehr als unbedingt notwendig dem Hausbau zu widmen und daher froh ist, wenn er die Modelle nur

they would far exceed the dimensions of the domestic train set and painfully remind the model builder of his limited means. The scale 1:87 applies at best to the height, but almost never to the length and depth of the building. Most of the single-family house models are actually about the size of roomy garden sheds. One would only be able to fit one single room per story if one were to really take the alleged scale seriously.

NEATLY AND TIDILY PRESSURE WASHED

A layman probably doesn't notice whether a model is true to scale or, like the vast majority of model train buildings, badly proportioned; most of them end up looking like toys despite all the fine detailing. Architects, on the other hand, look with contempt on the world of the Faller model buildings. The sterile to garish colorfulness and the greasy sheen of the dyed plastic assembly kit parts are deemed unpleasant. It is telling that these assembly kits are not offered in a neutral gray like the equally well-liked models of ships, planes, or tanks. Patina and dirt, chipped paint, and realistically imitated oil spots are

the sign of real mastery in this genre of model building. These are, however, seemingly matters that the normal H0er doesn't want to deal with. Otherwise the roofs would not be brick red, the window frames white, and the half-timbering so disgustingly brown that one could almost imagine a higher perfidious meaning behind it. The glued-together result therefore looks as clean and new as German villages present themselves in real life. It can be ruled out that the model buildings are actually trying to promote criticism of the German obsession with cleanliness and renovation. Thus, one must assume that the 1:87 hobbyist is just not interested in investing any more time than is absolutely necessary in building construction and is therefore happy when he only has to glue the parts together and not also paint them.

REALISM FORBIDDEN

It would be thinkable to introduce other model buildings into the market. For a while, the company Pola offered an ambitious range of urban buildings with highly decorated, industrial-era facades which were historically accurate both for the era

kleben und nicht auch noch bemalen muss.

UNTER REALISMUSVERBOT

Es wäre denkbar, andere Modell-bahnbauten auf den Markt zu bringen. Zeitweilig hat die Firma Pola ein anspruchsvolles Sortiment von Stadthäusern angeboten, die mit ihren Gründerzeitfassaden sowohl für die Ära der Dampfloks als auch für die Nachkriegszeit verwendet werden konnten. Auch das legendäre Modell „Brennendes Finanzamt" war ein Bausatz von Pola.
Doch selbst das ambitionierteste Modell würde sich in einem sehr wesentlichen Punkt von einem Archi-tekturmodell unterscheiden, in dem der Anspruch steckt, das geplante Bauwerk nicht lediglich abzubilden, sondern es zu interpretieren. Es gilt ein regelrechtes „Realismusverbot", das bis in die Architekturtheorie der Renaissance zurückverfolgt werden kann. Eine 600 Jahre alte Regel, die noch immer Gültigkeit hat! Der Verfasser der „Zehn Bücher über die Baukunst", Leon Battista Alberti (1404–1472), formulierte das Prinzip, „daß nämlich auf Glanz hergerichtete und sozusagen durch das Lockmittel

der Malerei aufgeputzte Modelle vorzuweisen nicht das Vorgehen eines Architekten ist […]. Deshalb soll man […] schlichte und einfache Modelle machen, an denen Du den Geist des Erfinders, nicht aber die Hand des Vorfertigers bewunderst." In dieser Forderung nach einfachen, abstrakten Modellen lässt sich das bis heute gültige Selbstverständnis des modernen Architekten erkennen. Dieser ist kein Handwerker mehr, sondern er steckt hinter der Konzep-tion und in den tatsächlich sichtba-ren Resultaten. Der Architekt will nicht darauf reduziert werden, nur für die gelungene Ausführung eines Bauwerks und ebenso wenig nur für die kunstvolle „Verfertigung" eines Modells verantwortlich sein. Vielmehr sieht er sich, nach den Worten Alber-tis, als der „Erfinder", der für seinen „Geist" bewundert werden will, nicht für das Werk seiner Hände.

MODELL MIT KLIMAANLAGE

Dem Alberti'schen „Abstraktionsge-bot", wie wir das Realismusverbot auch nennen können, sind wahr-scheinlich alle Architekturstudenten schon einmal begegnet, als ihm oder ihr ein Modell mit dem knappen

of the steam engine and the post-war period. The legendary model "burning tax office" was also a model from Pola.
But even the most ambitious model differentiates itself from an architec-tural model in that it not only seeks to portray the building, but also to interpret it. There is an outright "ban on reality" in architectural models which can be traced back to the architecture theory of the renais-sance. A 600-year-old rule that still applies! The author of the "Ten books on architecture," Leon Battista Alberti (1404–1472), formulated the principle "that the making of curious, polished models, with the delicacy of painting, is not required from an architect [...]. For this reason I would not have the models too exactly fin-ished, nor too delicate and neat, but plain and simple, more to be admired for the contrivance of the inventor than the hand of the workman." This demand for simple, abstract models is still apparent in the self-under-standing of modern architects today. The modern architect is no longer a workman, but is rather the force behind the conception and visible re-sults. The architect does not want to be reduced to just being responsible

for the successful completion of a building any more than for the artistic "production" of a model. He sees himself much more, in the words of Alberti, as the "inventor," who is admired for his "contrivance," not for the work of his hands.

MODEL WITH AIR CONDITIONING

The Albertine "abstraction rule," as we can also call the ban on realism, is probably known to every architec-ture student who has received their model back with the short verdict "doll house!" On the other side of the coin is the category "investor model," which is rather unpopular among architects but often unavoidable. In the history of the professional architecture models, there are only a few examples in which the reserva-tions towards dangerously strong realism have been ignored. These include models by Theodore Conrad, who is likely the only model builder to have had an obituary in the New York Times and whose models were examined by Teresa Fankhänel in her dissertation. Conrad worked for the major US American architecture offices of the 1950s and 60s. For a

Das Modell „Brennendes Finanzamt"
der Firma Pola rückt in Maßstabs-
treue und Wunschdenken sehr nah
heran an die Wirklichkeit
The model "burning tax office"
from the company Pola comes very
close to reality in scale and wishful
thinking

Urteil „Puppenstube!" zurückgege-
ben wurde. Andererseits gibt es die
Kategorie des „Investorenmodells",
das bei Architekten zwar unbeliebt,
aber oft nicht zu vermeiden ist. In
der Geschichte des professionel-
len Architekturmodells lassen sich
nur wenige Beispiele dafür finden,
dass der Vorbehalt gegenüber
einem gefährlich starken Realismus
aufgegeben wurde. Zu ihnen zählen
die Modelle von Theodore Conrad,
dem wohl einzigen Modellbauer, dem
die New York Times einen Nachruf
widmete und dessen Nachlass in der
Dissertation von Teresa Fankhänel
ausgewertet wurde. Conrad arbeitete für die großen US-amerikanischen
Architekturbüros der 1950er und
1960er Jahre. Für kurze Zeit galt es

als erstrebenswert, die technische
Perfektion der Rasterfassaden des
Nachkriegs-International-Style im
Modell mit exakt denselben Materia-
lien zu imitieren. Feinste Aluminium-
profile, Glas oder Acrylglas verwen-
dete man bei Modellen, die für eine
realistische Nachtansicht oft sogar
von innen beleuchtet waren. In einem
zeitgenössischen Zeitschriftenbei-
trag wurde berichtet, dass es Modelle gab, die eine eigene Klimaanlage
hatten, um nicht unter der Einwirkung
von hunderten Miniaturlampen in
Brand zu geraten.
Ein weiteres Beispiel für den größt-
möglichen Realismus im Architek-
turmodellbau ist die kurze Phase der
Modellsimulation mithilfe von spezi-
ellen Optiken und Videokameras in

short time, it was considered to be
desirable to imitate the technical per-
fection of the grid-like facades of the
post-war international style in models
with exactly the same building mate-
rials. Fine aluminum profiles, glass,
or acrylic were used in models; for a
realistic night impression, the models
were even frequently illuminated from
inside. A contemporary magazine
article reported that there were even
models with their own air condition-
ing in order to not burst into flames
from the effect of hundreds of miniature lamps.
A further example of the highest
possible degree of realism in architectural model construction is the
short phase of model simulation with
the help of special optics and video

cameras in the 1970s. The German
Architecture Museum was able to
secure a large collection of the Berlin
architect Ingo Wende's work, who
was a much sought after expert in
his time.

**ONE MILLION MODEL TRAIN
FANS ANNUALLY**

A construction history for model
train buildings has not yet been
written, even though significant
research work has now been
completed, at least for the era of
"märklinMODERNE." The history of
mentalities should not be neglected
in this. The only two books about
the history of model trains with
a cultural-historical orientation

Im Miniatur Wunderland Hamburg
muss man die Nachkriegsmoderne
schon gezielt suchen
At the Miniature Wonderland in
Hamburg one has to really look for
examples of post-war modernism

den 1970er Jahren. Das Deutsche
Architekturmuseum konnte hierzu
eine umfangreiche Sammlung von
Arbeiten des Berliner Architekten
Ingo Wende in seine Bestände auf-
nehmen, der seinerzeit ein gefragter
Experte war.

EINE MILLION MODELLBAHN-
FREUNDE, JÄHRLICH

Eine Baugeschichte des Modell-
bahnmodells ist bisher nicht
geschrieben worden, auch wenn
nun zumindest für die Epoche der
„märklinMODERNE" wesentliche
Quellenarbeit geleistet wurde. Die
Mentalitätsgeschichte sollte darin

nicht zu kurz kommen. Die beiden
einzigen kulturhistorisch orientierten Bücher zur Geschichte der
Modelleisenbahn von Bodo-Michael
Baumunk und Burkhard Spinnen
erschienen 1985 und 1998, da wäre
es doch wieder an der Zeit, einen
umfassenden Blick auf ein Genre
zu richten, dessen Faszination im
privaten Bereich sicherlich zurück-
geht – aber andererseits ist eine der
meistbesuchten Sehenswürdigkeiten
Hamburgs das Miniatur Wunderland,
die weltgrößte H0-Eisenbahnanlage
mit jährlich über einer Million Besuchern. Die Nachkriegsmoderne spielt
dort übrigens keine allzu große Rolle.

were published by Bodo-Michael
Baumunk and Burkhard Spinnen in
1985 and 1998. It thus might be high
time once again to cast a watchful
eye on this genre, even though its
appeal is certainly declining. On the
other hand, one of the most-visited
sights in Hamburg is the Miniature
Wonderland, the world's largest H0
model train set, with more than one
million visitors annually. Incidentally,
post-war modernism does not play a
very significant role there.

„Es war ein Akt der Befreiung"
"It was an act of liberation"

DER PLAKATKÜNSTLER KLAUS STAECK ÜBER EINE HALBE VILLA UND EINE GANZ GROSSE IDEE

POSTER ARTIST KLAUS STAECK ON HALF A VILLA AND A GREAT BIG IDEA

Von Zeit zu Zeit bleibt Klaus Staeck auf dem Weg zu seinem Heidelberger Atelierladen am Hauptbahnhof stehen. Er wirft ein, zwei Euro in den Modellbahnautomaten, freut sich an den kleinen sausenden Zügen und ertappt sich bei dem Gedanken: „Hoffentlich stoßen sie jetzt nicht zusammen!" International bekannt wurde der 1938 geborene Grafikdesigner, der Ausbildung nach ernsthafter Jurist, als politischer Plakatkünstler. 1972 gestaltete er ein damals aufsehenerregendes Plakat zur Bundestagswahl – mit der Überschrift: „Deutsche Arbeiter! Die SPD will euch eure Villen im Tessin wegnehmen". Die darunter abgebildete Villa erscheint vielen Modellbahnern wohlbekannt, erinnert sie doch an den Faller-Bausatz „Villa im Tessin". Was das eine mit dem anderen zu tun hat (oder eben nicht), erklärt Klaus Staeck im Gespräch mit dem Theologen Matthias Ludwig:

From time to time, Klaus Staeck stops in front of the main train station on his way to his Heidelberg atelier. He puts a euro or two in the model railway machine, enjoys the little rushing trains, and catches himself thinking: "I hope they don't collide!" The graphic designer, who was born in 1938, actually trained to become a lawyer, but became internationally known through his work as a political poster artist. In 1972, he designed what was then a provocative poster for the parliamentary elections with the motto "German workers! The SPD wants to take away your villas in Ticino." The villa pictured below was familiar to many model railway enthusiasts; it reminded them of the Faller assembly kit "Villa in Ticino." Klaus Staeck explains what one has to do with the other (or not) in a discussion with theologian Matthias Ludwig:

Matthias Ludwig [ML] *Herr Staeck, wie kam es zu diesem Plakat?*
Klaus Staeck [KS] Entstanden ist die Idee bei einem Krankenhausaufenthalt. Wegen des Verdachts auf Hirnblutung wurde ich in die Neurologie eingewiesen. Dort hat man mich punktiert. Schon bei dem Wort hätte ich hellhörig werden sollen. Es hieß: „Das regeneriert sich in 24 Stunden." Bei mir regenerierte sich erst mal gar nichts. Also musste ich mich irgendwie retten – durch eine Plakatidee. In dieser körperlichen Hochspannung, wie ich sie nicht wieder erlebt habe, arbeitete ich die ganze Zeit an der „Villa im Tessin".
ML *Was war 1972 der konkrete politische Hintergrund?*
KS Im Wahlkampf, Willy Brandt kandidierte, gab es sehr unfaire Angriffe. Der SPD, der ich damals schon angehörte, wurde in großformatigen Anzeigen unterstellt, sie würde „der Oma ihr klein Häuschen" wegnehmen. Was macht man gegen diese Ungeheuerlichkeit? Man muss das ins Absurde treiben! Die „Villa im Tessin" war ein geflügeltes Wort für Neureichentum. Deshalb nahm ich dieses Bild und verband es mit den „Deutschen Arbeitern" in einer an die Nazi-Zeit erinnernden Schrift.

Der Plakatkünstler Klaus Staeck und die „Villa im Tessin"
The poster artist Klaus Staeck and the "Villa in Ticino"

ML *Die „Villa" auf Ihrem Plakat ist in Wirklichkeit ein Stuttgarter Appartementhaus, das der in China gebürtige Architekt Chen Kuen Lee hier von 1960 bis 1961 umsetzte. Wie kamen Sie auf diesen Bau?*
KS Mit Gerd Steidl, der damals alle meine Plakate verlegt hat, wälzte ich Architekturbände. Ich glaube, er kam auf die Idee, aus einem der Bücher diese Villa zu nehmen. Sie war aber für unsere Verhältnisse ein bisschen groß, wir brauchten ja Platz für den Text. Deshalb haben wir eine Etage weggenommen, haben die Villa „kupiert".
ML *Stimmt es, dass Sie eigentlich Architekt werden wollten?*

Matthias Ludwig [ML] *Mr. Staeck, what is the story behind this poster?*
Klaus Staeck [KS] The idea came about while I was in the hospital. I was sent to the neurology department with a suspected cerebral hemorrhage. They punctured me. My ears should have perked up at the word. They said: "you'll be better in 24 hours." But nothing got better right away. I had to distract myself—through a poster idea. I was in a state of extreme physical tension, like I've never experienced since. And in that period, I worked on the "Villa in Ticino."
ML *What was the concrete political background in 1972?*

KS In the election there were very unfair attacks; Willy Brandt was a candidate. I was a member of the SPD back then. Large-format advertisements alleged that the SPD was going to take "grandma's little house" away. What can you do against this atrocity? You have to push it to the point of absurdity! The "Villa in Ticino" was an expression for new money. And for that reason, I used this image and connected with the "German workers," a phrase reminiscent of the Nazi times.
ML *The "villa" on your poster is actually an apartment house in Stuttgart which was designed by Chinese born architect Chen Kuen Lee be-*

KS In der DDR seinerzeit – ich bin in Bitterfeld groß geworden – musste man vor dem Abitur drei Berufswünsche angeben. Als erstes Filmregisseur, das hatte gar keine Chance. Als zweites Architekt. Und als drittes, zur Not, Kunstlehrer. Ich wurde auch nach Weimar eingeladen zur Aufnahmeprüfung für das Architekturstudium. Wie sich nachher herausstellte, wurde ich aus politischen Gründen nicht genommen. Aber ich habe die Architekten immer bewundert, weil sie diese kleinen Modelle gebaut haben.

ML *Wie wurde Ihr Plakat aufgenommen?*

tween 1960 and 1961. *How did you choose this particular building?*

KS I used to pore over architecture books with Gerd Steidl, who published all of my posters back then. I think he came up with the idea to select this villa from one of those books. For our purposes it was actually a bit big; we needed space for

Zwischenstopp am Modellbahnautomaten im Heidelberger Hauptbahnhof: Matthias Ludwig auf dem Weg zum Interview
Stopping for a moment at the Heidelberg main station: Matthias Ludwig on the way to the interview

the text. That's why we removed one story; we "cropped" the villa.

ML *Is it true that you actually wanted to become an architect?*

KS I grew up in Bitterfeld. Back then in the GDR, you had to name three career choices before you started high school. My first choice was film director; no chance. My second choice was architect. And my third, if need be, art teacher. I was even invited to Weimar to take the architecture qualifying examination. As I found out later, I wasn't accepted for political reasons. But I always admired architects because they built these little models.

ML *How was your poster received?*

KS It was an act of liberation. And it is my most well-known poster with a printrun of 70,000. Nearly all were posted. At my age, you begin to ask yourself: what will remain from all the things you've done in your life? I'm sure that it's this poster. I travel often with the train, and even today people ask me "aren't you the one who did that poster about the villa in Ticino?"

ML *What is the connection between your poster and the assembly kit "Villa in Ticino"?*

KS I only learned later that this model for model train enthusiasts

Deutsche Arbeiter!
Die SPD will euch eure Villen im Tessin wegnehmen

LINKS „Deutsche Arbeiter! Die SPD will euch eure Villen im Tessin wegnehmen" – so der Text des Staeck-Plakats aus dem Jahr 1972
LEFT "German workers! The SPD wants to take your villas in Ticino away from you"—states the Staeck poster from the year 1972

UNTEN Die Stuttgarter Villa, die als Motiv für das Staeck-Plakat diente
BELOW The Stuttgart villa that served as the image for the Staeck poster

KS Es war ein Akt der Befreiung. Und es ist mein bekanntestes Plakat mit einer Auflage von 70.000 Stück. Fast alle wurden auch geklebt. In meinem Alter kann man sich ja schon mal der Frage stellen: Was überlebt von all den Dingen, die du gemacht hast? Ich bin sicher, es ist dieses Plakat. Heute noch – ich bin sehr viel mit der Bahn unterwegs – gibt es immer mindestens einen, der kommt und sagt: „Sind Sie nicht der mit der Villa im Tessin?"

ML *Was verbindet Ihr Plakat mit dem Modellbausatz „Villa im Tessin"?*

KS Ich habe erst später erfahren, dass es eine Art Nachbau für Modelleisenbahnliebhaber gibt. Die „Villa im Tessin" bietet sich an als Metapher für die Nachkriegszeit, für den Wiederaufbau. Da schwingt so viel mit: Italien als Traumreiseland, zumindest das Tessin als die nächste Station von Deutschland aus gesehen. Das Wohlstandsversprechen, sich im Tessin niederlassen zu können.

ML *Sie sind gar kein Modelleisenbahner?*

KS Ich habe selber auch mal Modelleisenbahnen gehabt. Aber ich brachte es nur auf wenige Wagen und Schienen. Die Wohnung war nicht so groß und nicht geeignet. Ich habe immer bei anderen bewundert, mit welcher Energie sie dieses Hobby betrieben haben. Modelleisenbahn ist für mich eine Erinnerung an die Kindheit und eine Werbung für das Bahnfahren.

ML *Sie sind bekennender Bahnfahrer. In den neun Jahren als Präsident der Akademie der Künste pendelten Sie mit dem Zug zwischen Heidelberg und Berlin. Hat es Sie auch schon ins Tessin gezogen?*

KS Tatsächlich bin ich neulich mit meiner Frau ins Tessin in den Urlaub gefahren – auf dieser wunderbaren Bahnstrecke durch die Alpen. Gegenüber von uns bemühte sich eine Mutter verzweifelt, ihrem Kind einen Blick zu entlocken: „Guck doch mal, die wunderbare Natur, dieser Wasserfall, da liegt schon Schnee auf den Bergen!" Das Kind dachte gar nicht daran, auch nur einen Moment von seinem Handy aufzuschauen. Was ich im Zug schon alles an Geschichten erfahren habe. Die Bahn steckt voller Geschichten.

existed. The "Villa in Ticino" is a good metaphor for the post-war years, for reconstruction. There are so many issues wrapped up in there: Italy as a vacation destination, at least Ticino as the nearest station from a German perspective. And the promise of prosperity, that one would be able to settle in Ticino.

ML *Are you a model railway enthusiast?*

KS Yes, I had model trains at one time. But I only had a few cars and rails. The apartment wasn't very big and not well suited for the hobby. I always marveled at the others—the energy that they put into this hobby! For me, model trains are a reminder of my childhood and an advertisement for taking the real train.

ML *You have already mentioned that you enjoy riding trains. In the nine years that you were the president of the Academy of Arts in Berlin, you commuted by train between Heidelberg and Berlin. Have you also made it to Ticino?*

KS Yes, I actually went on vacation to Ticino with my wife—on this wonderful train track through the Alps. Across from us, a mother tried desperately to get her child to look out: "look at the wonderful nature, that waterfall. There's snow on the mountains!" The child didn't think to look up from their cell phone for even a moment. I have experienced so many stories in the train. The train is full of stories.

Atlantis im Wohnzimmerformat
Atlantis in living room size

CHRISTIAN HOLL

ALLTAGSARCHITEKTUR AUF DER MODELLBAHNPLATTE

EVERYDAY ARCHITECTURE ON THE MODEL RAILWAY BOARD

Wenn von Modelleisenbahnen die Rede ist, stellen sich meist Bilder von idyllischen Landschaften mit mittelalterlich anmutenden Stadtversatzstücken ein. Vermutlich wurde diese Vorstellung nie besser umgesetzt als mit der Insel Lummerland aus „Jim Knopf und Lukas der Lokomotivführer", das (nach dem Kinderbuch von Michael Ende) 1961/62 von der Augsburger Puppenkiste inszeniert wurde. Aus der Begrenzung der Modellbahnplatte wurden Meeresufer und Sandstrand. Es finden sich die Zutaten, die in der Regel Modelleisenbahnen prägen: Berge, Tunnels, ein Schloss, wenige Häuser und natürlich ein Bahnhof – ein friedliches Kinder-Utopia, ein Atlantis im Wohnzimmerformat. Diese heile Welt, die sich nach dem Trauma des Zweiten Weltkriegs als eskapistischer Rückzugsort im Hobbykeller verwirklichen ließ, ist freilich nicht die ganze Wahrheit.

When one talks about model railways, most people imagine idyllic landscapes with medieval-looking city models. This image was probably best implemented in 1961/62 by the Augsburger Puppenkiste, namely the island Lummerland from "Jim Knopf and Lukas the Train Conductor" from the children's book by Michael Ende. The edge of the model railway board became the seashore and a sandy beach. There are all the ingredients which usually characterize model train sets: mountains, tunnels, a castle, a few houses, and naturally a train station—a friendly child-utopia, an Atlantis in living room size. This ideal world, which was realized as an escapist refuge in the hobby room after the trauma of the Second World War, is however not the whole truth of the matter.

„Lummerland" aus der Augsburger
Puppenkiste
"Lummerland" from the Augsburger
Puppenkiste

DIE ANDERE HÄLFTE DER WAHRHEIT

Die Modelleisenbahn war ebenso Abbild einer realen Traumwelt – mit einem Versprechen auf eine bessere Zukunft, die in engem Verhältnis zum Alltag der jungen Bundesrepublik stand. Die Bausätze nahmen sich keine außergewöhnlichen, heraus-ragenden Architekturbeispiele zum Vorbild. Vielmehr orientierten sie sich gerade an typischen Bauten, die der Alltagserfahrung entsprachen. Sie zeigten, was die Menschen schon in ähnlicher Form gesehen hatten und sich in ihrer Umgebung vorstellen konnten. Denn Architektur ist keine autonome Entscheidung, weder von ihren Architekten, noch von ihren

THE OTHER HALF OF THE TRUTH

Model train sets were also an image of the real dream world—the promise of a better future which was closely related to daily life in the young Federal Republic. The assembly kits were not based on unusual or prominent architectural examples, but were instead oriented towards typical buildings from everyday life. They showed buildings similar to those that people had already seen, and which they could imagine in their surroundings. Architecture is not an autonomous decision—not by the architects and not by the client either. It is embedded in wider social models, is part of the collective imagination of a good life. It is inter-

Bauherren. Sie ist eingebunden in gesellschaftliche Leitbilder, ist Teil von kollektiven Vorstellungen von einem guten Leben. Sie ist verwoben mit politischen Prozessen und sozialen Mechanismen. Das gilt besonders in der Alltagswelt – sie überführt zunächst singuläre Neuerungen in vielfachen Abwandlungen in eine Routine, die als Teil eines kollektiven Einverständnisses unhinterfragt akzeptiert wird.

Unter der Architektur des Alltäglichen wird hier in erster Linie eine verstanden, die auf Rezeptwissen beruht. Dieses bewährt sich bei Aufgaben, die regelmäßig wiederkehrend und in großer Zahl auftreten. Darin sind Regeln gespeichert, die nicht hinterfragt werden müssen, weil sie sich bereits bei ähnlichen Problemen bewährt haben oder kollektiv geteilten Leitbildern und Sehnsüchten entsprechen. Die Bausätze, die für die Modelleisenbahnlandschaften angeboten wurden, bestätigen dieses Einverständnis. Wer sein Modell in großer Zahl verkaufen wollte, musste zum einen darauf setzen, dass diese Architektur von den Käufern als typisch, als alltäglich erkannt werden konnte. Zum anderen wird ein solcher Typ

dadurch wirkmächtiger, dass er als Musterlösung für eine bestimmte Frage gilt, als Materialisierung einer Sehnsucht, eines Leitbilds: Die Landschaft mit ihren Elementen wird nicht nur als typische in einem Modell umgesetzt. Diese Miniatur-Idylle wird wiederum zum Horizont dessen, was in der echten Welt gesucht wird und dort verwirklicht werden soll. Die Grenzen zwischen Vorbild und Abbild verschwimmen – bis hinein in die politische Sphäre.

LUDWIG II. IM WESTENTASCHENFORMAT

So wirkte die „Villa im Tessin" wie eine High-End-Version des massentauglichen Bungalows und war damit Teil einer Alltagsrealität, die sogar eines Regierungssitzes für würdig erachtet wurde. Der Bonner Kanzlerbungalow von Sep Ruf, den Ludwig Erhard in Auftrag gegeben hatte, adelte weniger das moderne Wohnhaus als Regierungsbau; vielmehr versinnbildlichte er die Verwurzelung der Politik im Alltag und verschränkte demonstrativ die Sphäre des Wohnens mit der des Politischen. Mit ihrer Referenz an US-amerikanische Vorbilder standen

woven with political processes and social mechanisms. This is particularly true of the day-to-day world; individual innovations are repeated, eventually becoming a new routine and subsequently part of a collective self-understanding which is accepted without question.

Day-to-day architecture is one which is based on a knowledge of recipes. This knowledge is maintained through a large number of regularly repeated tasks. This process contains a range of rules which do not need to be questioned, since they have been proved in other situations or correspond to collectively shared models and aspirations. The assembly kits which were offered for model train landscapes confirm this understanding. Producers who wanted to sell a large number of their models needed to ensure that the architecture of the models would be recognized as typical and everyday by the buyers. This, however, increases the impact of such a type as a typical solution for a particular question, as the materialization of an aspiration, a social model. The landscape and its elements are not just typical in the model world. This miniature idyll becomes in turn the

horizon for what is striven for and implemented in the real world. The boundaries between the example and its reproduction blur—right into the political sphere.

LUDWIG THE SECOND IN MINIATURE

The "Villa in Ticino" appeared as a high-end version of the mass market bungalow and was thus part of a daily reality that was even considered worthy of the seat of government. The Chancellor Bungalow in Bonn, which was commissioned to Sep Ruf by Ludwig Erhard, was less of an attempt to elevate the modern house to the level of a government building and more of a symbol of the rooting of politics in everyday life and demonstratively intertwined the spheres of living and politics. With their reference to US-American models, bungalows represented a fulfillment of the promise of prosperity: large window areas created a new connection with the outdoors which was weather-independent. Domestic appliances and open designs with flowing sequences of rooms promised a freeing from traditional middle-class norms. The everyday

Spitzendeckchen unterm Flachdach, oder: Wenn der Alltag auf
den Modernitätsanspruch traf –
Hannelore Kohl 1987 im Bonner
Kanzlerbungalow
Lace doilies under a flat roof, or:
when daily life meets modernist
aspirations—Hannelore Kohl in
the Chancellor Bungalow in Bonn
in 1987

Bungalows für das eingelöste Wohlstandsversprechen: Große Scheiben stellten einen neuartigen, von der Witterung unabhängigen Außenbezug her. Hausmaschinen und ein offenes Wohnen mit fließenden Räumfolgen versprachen die Defrei ung von überkommenen bürgerlichen Normvorstellungen. Diese Alltagsversion von Neutras Prärie-Häusern oder den Case-Study-Houses des Architektenehepaars Eames versprach alle Möglichkeiten des modernen Lebens. Beim Bungalow ist der enge Bezug zum „american way of life" offensichtlich – nicht nur in der Bundesrepublik war dies ein kaum hinterfragter Orientierungspunkt. In der „Villa im Tessin" kreuzt sich dieses Ideal mit einer anderen Entwicklung: der des Südens als populärem Urlaubsziel, das im Tessin und später in der Toskana mit einem gewissen Bildungshabitus gelebt wurde.

Eines macht die gedrängte Modelleisenbahnlandschaft, in der die prägenden Elemente in strenger Auswahl dicht aneinandergerückt werden mussten, besonders interessant: die Art, wie Versatzstücke typischerweise kombiniert wurden. Hier verbindet sich romantische

Idylle (Berge, Tannen, Fachwerkhäuser) geradezu notwendigerweise mit einer technischen Komponente (der der Eisenbahn). Hier wird die (vermeintlich) zeitlose Ideallandschaft mit dem Konzept des Fortschritts überlagert. Überspitzt könnte man sagen, dass sich jeder Modelleisenbahner als Ludwig II. im Westentaschenformat gerieren konnte – hatte doch auch der Bayernkönig gerne vergangenheitsselige Traumwelten mit neuer Technik kombiniert.

Diese Spannung fand sich im Alltag wieder – freilich um das Maß weniger tiefgründig, das es erlaubt, an dieser Spannung nicht verzweifeln oder leiden zu müssen. Denn auch das gehört zum Wesen des Alltäglichen: dass es einen Umgang mit den widersprüchlichen Anforderungen und Erwartungen eröffnet. Wer plant und baut, weiß, wie schwierig es ist, kurzfristige und langfristige Ziele, gesellschaftliche und individuelle Wünsche und zudem noch wirtschaftliche Möglichkeiten auf einmal zu berücksichtigen. Die Modelleisenbahn vermittelt in diesem Widerspruch, indem sie eine leichter beherrschbare und gestaltbare Alternative zur Wirklichkeit anbietet (weswegen sie auch möglichst „echt" auszusehen

version of Neutra's prairie houses or the Eames' case study houses promised all of the opportunities of modern life. In bungalows, the close relationship to the "American way of life" is apparent—an unquestioned point of reference, not only in the Federal Republic. In the "Villa in Ticino," this ideal meets another development: the south as a popular vacation destination, which first in Ticino, and later in Tuscany was enjoyed with a particular cultivated habitus.

One thing makes the crowded model train landscape, in which characterizing elements are strictly selected and arranged in close proximity to one another, particularly interesting: the way in which models are typically combined. Here, the romantic idyll (mountains, evergreens, half-timbered houses) is almost necessarily combined with a technical component (that of the train). The concept of progress is then superimposed on this (apparently) timeless ideal landscape. To exaggerate, one could say that the model railway builder acts like Ludwig the second in miniature—the Bavarian king also enjoyed combining dream worlds of the past with new technology.

This tension is also reflected in everyday life—of course reduced to a degree that does not produce undue distress. This is also an aspect of the essence of daily life: that it opens up an interaction between contradicting requirements and expectations. Anyone who plans and builds will know how difficult it is to simultaneously consider short- and long-term goals, social and individual desires, and, on top of it all, the possibilities offered by the individual financial situation. Models trains mediate this contradiction by offering a more easily manageable and designable alternative to reality (which is also why it needs to look as "real" as possible). At the same time, it offers a window into an ideal that could resolve these contradictions in reality. In this aspect, the boundaries between the example and its reproduction are again blurred.

IN A NEW LIGHT

This view onto the "everydayness" of model railways could contribute to the casting of post-war modernism in a new light. One frequently gets the impression that architecture and urban design are dominated by a type

hat, um zu wirken). Gleichzeitig bietet sie ein Fenster auf eine Weltvorstellung, die diese Widersprüche dann in der Realität einlösen könnte. Auch hierin werden die Grenzen zwischen Abbild und Vorbild aufgeweicht.

IN EINEM NEUEN LICHT

Ein solcher Blick auf die Alltäglichkeit der Modelleisenbahn könnte dazu beitragen, die Nachkriegsmoderne in einem anderen Licht erscheinen zu lassen. Vielfach entsteht der Eindruck, dass die architektonische und städtebauliche Wirklichkeit von einer vergangenheitsvergessenen Moderne beherrscht sei. Doch dies ist nur ein kleiner Ausschnitt, bestimmt von herausragenden Arbeiten und Einzelfällen. Wir sollten es uns aber gönnen – mit Blick auf den Alltag, der uns in den Modelleisenbahnen so offensichtlich als Melange von Wirklichkeit und Wunschbild entgegentritt – die Nachkriegszeit differenzierter zu sehen. Wir sollten neben

den neuesten architektonischen und städtebaulichen Entwicklungen auch das als den ureigenen Teil der Nachkriegsmoderne akzeptieren, was sich in der Modell-Idylle unverstellt offenbart. Die darin sichtbare Widersprüchlichkeit war ein grundlegender Teil des damaligen Alltags – und ist nicht minder Teil der unsrigen, wenn auch in anderem Kleid. Möglicherweise ist es gerade das, was die Nachkriegszeit als eine besondere Form der Moderne kennzeichnet: wie in ihr neue Architektur und vertraute Landschaft, Technik und Sehnsucht, Fachwerkhaus und „Villa im Tessin" zusammengehören.

of modernism which has forgotten the past. This is however only a small proportion, determined by excellent works and individual examples. We should, however, allow ourselves to see post-war modernism in a more differentiated way—with a view to the day-to-day life that the model train presents as an obvious melange of reality and ideals. In addition to the newest architectural and urban design developments, we should also accept what is genuinely revealed in the model idyll as an integral part of post-war modernism. The discrepancies visible there were a fundamental part of daily life back then—and are also an equally significant part of our daily life today, even if they take a different form. Perhaps this is exactly the aspect which makes post-war modernism a special form of modernism: the way it brings together new architecture and the familiar landscape, technology and aspirations, half-timbered houses and the "Villa in Ticino."

Bahnparade vor dem Bahnhof Kehl
im Märklin-Magazin 4/1969
A parade of trains in front of the
Kehl station in the Märklin-Magazin
4/1969

Ein „baugeschichtliches Diorama" im Kinderzimmer
An "architectural history diorama" in the children's bedroom

DER ARCHITEKTURKRITIKER FALK JAEGER ÜBER ARCHITEKTUR, MODELLEISENBAHNEN UND SÄGEMEHL

ARCHITECTURE CRITIC FALK JAEGER ON ARCHITECTURE, MODEL RAILWAYS, AND SAWDUST

Die Szenerie wirkt wie auf einer Eisenbahnanlage: Zum Gespräch über seine Modellbahn aus Jugendtagen treffen wir den Architekturkritiker Falk Jaeger in seinem Haus. Er lebt und arbeitet in einem Wohngebäude aus den 1930er Jahren, das einstöckig mit Zeltdach wie der Prototyp eines klassischen Einfamilienhauses wirkt. Zwischen Wannsee und der von Berlin nach Potsdam führenden Bahnlinie gelegen, thront es auf einem Hang. Aus dem Wohnzimmer heraus schauen wir auf ein Waldstück, durch das sich im Zehn-Minuten-Takt die S-Bahn schlängelt. Jaegers Hang zur Modellbahnromantik rührt aus Kindertagen. Der 1950 geborene Publizist und Hochschullehrer hat sich mit der Modellbahn schon früh „auch architektonisch betätigt". Zu seinen ersten bauhistorischen Überblickswerken gehörten die Kataloge von Faller, Kibri und Co. „Da war die ganze Geschichte der Architektur wunderschön ausgebreitet", erinnert

The scenery feels like a model railway board. We met architecture critic Falk Jaeger at his house to talk about the model train set of his youth. He lives and works in a house from the 1930s; the one story with a peaked roof feels like the prototype of a classic single-family house. Located between Wannsee and the train line between Berlin and Potsdam, the house sits high up on a hillside. The living room looks out on a forest through which the S-bahn meanders every ten minutes. Jaeger's inclination to model railway romanticism stems from his childhood. The publicist and university lecturer, who was born in 1950, got "architecturally involved" with the model railway in early years. Catalogs from Faller, Kibri, and others were some of the first architectural history overview works that he studied. "The whole history of architecture was wonderfully presented there." He reminisces in a discussion with art historian Ralf Liptau:

Der Architekturkritiker Falk Jaeger
im Gespräch mit Ralf Liptau
Architecture critic Falk Jaeger
discusses with Ralf Liptau

er sich im Gespräch mit dem Kunsthistoriker Ralf Liptau:

*Ralf Liptau [RL] Herr Jaeger, wann
hatten Sie die erste Anlage?*
Falk Jaeger [FJ] Ich habe mit sieben
Jahren die ersten Gleise bekommen,
einen Zug mit Dampflok und einen
Bahnhof. Drei Jahre später hatte ich
schon eine größere Anlage, die ich
immer um Weihnachten für ein paar
Wochen aufgebaut habe. Die Familie
war dann bereit, um die Anlage

herumzutanzen. Als ich ein eigenes
Zimmer hatte, wurde die Anlage
noch größer, immerhin gut drei Meter
lang. Da habe ich sozusagen unter
der Anlage geschlafen.
*RL Welche Rolle spielten hier Archi-
tektur und Stadt?*
FJ Mich hat immer interessiert, nicht
nur die Lokomotiven fahren zu lassen, sondern ein Diorama zu bauen
aus Stadt und Landschaft. Es gab
immer eine mehr ländliche und eine
mehr städtische Ecke. Mit 13 oder

*Ralf Liptau [RL] Mr. Jaeger, when
did you get your first model train
set?*
Falk Jaeger [FJ] When I was seven
years old, I received tracks, a train
with a steam engine, and a train
station. Three years later, I had a
larger set, which I set up for a few
weeks around Christmas. The family
was prepared to step around the
model train set for that limited time
period once a year. When I got my
own room, the set got even bigger,

at least three meters long. I more or
less slept under it.
*RL What role did architecture and
urban design play?*
FJ I was always interested in not
only in the trains, but also building a
diorama of the city and its landscape.
There was always one part that was
more rural and one part that was more
urban. When I was 13 or 14, I per-
fected that even further. At various
points, I made the entire board into
a snowy landscape by dusting it with

Falk Jaeger um 1961 vor seiner
zimmerfüllenden Modellbahnanlage
Falk Jaeger around 1961 with his
room-filling model train set

14 Jahren habe ich das dann weiter perfektioniert. Ich hatte zeitweise die komplette Anlage als Schneelandschaft, die mit Mehl bestäubt war, dann eine Wüstenlandschaft mit Sägemehl. Dann habe ich eine klassische mitteleuropäische Stadt gebaut, mit einem historischen Stadtkern, einer Stadterweiterung aus dem späten 19. Jahrhundert und moderneren Infrastrukturanlagen, also zum Beispiel einem Postgebäude aus den 1960ern.

RL Das heißt, Sie haben die Stadt als etwas Gewachsenes verstanden und dargestellt?

FJ Ja. Mit etwa 13 Jahren verstand ich natürlich noch nicht so viel von Architektur und Stadtplanung. Wir hatten aber einen tollen Volksschullehrer, der uns in Heimatkunde, so hieß das damals, die Baugeschichte nahe gebracht hat. Wie sich eine Stadt strukturiert, hatte ich damals offenbar schon begriffen.

RL Modelleisenbahner stehen ja im Ruf, ziemlich konservativ zu sein und sich zu Hause ihre eigene Welt zu bauen. Wie passt da moderne Architektur rein? Welche Rolle hatte sie in Ihrer Anlage?

FJ Eisenbahner freuen sich mehr über historische Bauten. Ich wollte aber

flour, then a desert with sawdust. Then I built a classical central European city with a historical city center, a city expansion from the late 19th century, and modern infrastructure, for example a post office from the 1960s.

RL So you understood and designed the city as something which evolved?

FJ Yes. At the age of 13, I didn't understand a lot about architecture and urban planning. We had a really good elementary teacher though who taught us local heritage, that was what it was called back then, and who taught us about architectural history. I had apparently already understood back then how a city is structured.

RL Model railway builders have a reputation for being conservative and for building their own world at home. How does modern architecture fit into all of this? What role did it have in your first model train set?

FJ Model train builders enjoy historical buildings more. But I wanted to build a city that reflected reality to some degree; for that reason, I incorporated modern buildings as well. Nevertheless, the old houses and barns were my real passion. The new ones were a necessity.

RL Was it already a sign of postmodernism that a budding architecture critic built a historical city in the 1960s?

FJ I wouldn't go that far, but nevertheless: at first, I wanted to go into monument protection. I ended up studying architecture with a focus on architectural history. I grew up in Esslingen, in a medieval city. I internalized that somehow as a child. Then when I was studying in the 1970s, it was a period in which everyone was thinking about monument protection very intensely in general, and in which monument protection laws were put into place.

RL So you would say that your own model railway building did not have a strong influence on your career path?

FJ No, it did implicitly, because it made me notice architecture at an early age. I would look through catalogs by Faller, etc. and form my own concept about the eras of architectural history up until the present. I was, for example, very interested in the legendary villa in Ticino, because it was available as a model. I couldn't afford it though. But I had the famous mountain chapel from Falzarego on top of my mountain. At some point,

eine Stadt bauen, die einigermaßen eine Realität darstellt und deshalb auch moderne Bauten braucht. Trotzdem war mein Herzblut eher bei den alten Häusern und Schuppen. Die neuen mussten halt sein.

RL Kündigt sich da schon die Postmoderne an, wenn ein angehender Architekturkritiker in den 1960ern die historische Stadt baut?

FJ Soweit würde ich nicht gehen, aber dennoch: Ich wollte ja erst Denkmalpfleger werden, Architektur

mit dem Schwerpunkt Baugeschichte habe ich dann studiert. Ich bin in Esslingen aufgewachsen, in einer mittelalterlichen Stadt. Das habe ich als Kind wohl in mich aufgesogen. Als ich in den 70ern studiert habe, war das ja eine Zeit, in der man allgemein über den Denkmalschutz sehr intensiv nachdachte und Denkmalschutzgesetze initiierte.

RL Der Einfluss des Modellbahnbaus auf die eigene Laufbahn war also nicht so stark?

two years later, I was actually there and had a look at the original. I was completely ecstatic.

RL Were there real situations that you copied exactly in parts of your set?

FJ No. I had a pretty good idea of how a historical city center looked and I built it myself out of paper. It was also a financial problem, buying all of the house assembly kits that were available myself. When I build up a new set in the near future, I'm

OBEN Mal Wüstenstadt, mal Altstadt auf der einstigen Modellbahnanlage Falk Jaegers
ABOVE A desert town here, a historical town there on Falk Jaeger's model railway set-up at the time

FJ Implizit schon, denn es hat mich früh auf Architektur aufmerksam gemacht. Man hat ja die schönen Kataloge von Faller usw. gewälzt und sich ein eigenes Bild über die Epochen der Architekturgeschichte bis in die Gegenwart geformt. Mich hat zum Beispiel die legendäre Villa im Tessin interessiert, weil es die als Modell gab. Die habe ich mir aber nicht kaufen können. Aber die Bergkapelle, die berühmte auf dem Falzarego, die hatte ich auch auf meinem Berg oben stehen. Irgendwann, zwei Jahre später, war ich dann auch wirklich mal dort und habe mir das Original angeschaut. Da war ich ganz verzückt.

RL *Gab es andere exakte Vorbilder für Teile ihrer Anlage?*

FJ Nein. Wie eine Altstadt aussah, das wusste ich einigermaßen und habe sie selbst aus Papier gebaut.

Es wäre ja auch ein finanzielles Problem gewesen, sich alle Häuser, die es als Bausatz gab, selbst zu kaufen. Wenn ich demnächst wieder mal eine Anlage aufbaue, kaufe ich mir einen 3-D-Drucker und drucke die Bauten, die ich haben will, einfach selbst aus. Heute ist man nicht mehr auf die Angebotspalette der Hersteller angewiesen.

RL *Und was werden das dann für Häuser sein?*

FJ Die Villa Savoye von Le Corbusier würde ich wahrscheinlich drucken und dann Stadthäuser, die aussehen wie von Erich Mendelsohn. Da hätte ich schon ausreichend Ideen. Ich würde wieder ein baugeschichtliches Diorama entwickeln. Und das jetzt, 50 Jahre später, natürlich mit weiteren Bauten auch aus der jüngsten Architekturgeschichte.

going to buy a 3D printer and print out the pieces that I want myself. Today, you're no longer bound by what producers can offer.

RL *And what kinds of buildings will they be?*

FJ I would probably print the Villa Savoye from Le Corbusier and then townhouses that look like they are from Erich Mendelsohn. I have plenty of ideas. I would develop an architectural history diorama again. And this time, 50 years later, I would also naturally incorporate buildings from the earliest chapters of architectural history.

Hamburger Modelle
Hamburg models

JÖRG SCHILLING

WAS BLEIBT VOM CITY-HOF?

WHAT REMAINS OF CITY-HOF?

Es gibt auch einen Flughafen, ab und zu startet sogar ein unbekanntes Flugobjekt. Im Hamburger Miniatur Wunderland ist vieles möglich und doch ist Utopie hier ein Fremdwort. Urbane Kultur wird in diesem Modellbau-Eldorado zwar minimiert und komprimiert, aber erstaunlich authentisch mit allen Facetten der Massengesellschaft dargestellt: das Menschengedränge auf dem Flohmarkt unter dem U-Bahn-Viadukt, der Polizeieinsatz vor dem Fußballstadion oder die Tänzergruppen auf den Trucks einer Love-Parade. Lebensechte Arrangements führen das eventgebeutelte Großstadtleben vor Augen. Romantisiert wird höchstens das Naturhafte – wie die Pappmaché-Gebirge der nachgestellten Alpen. Nebenan erhebt sich hinter einer Gründerzeitruine bereits das Stahlbetonskelett eines neuen Bahnhofs. Und der Besucher blickt in eine alte, zum Erlebnisbad aufgerüstete Schwimmhalle. Umwandlungsprozesse sind Teil der Modellbau-Inszenierung.

There is even an airport. Every once in a while, an unknown flying object starts up. Many things are possible at the Miniature Wonderland in Hamburg, and yet utopia is a foreign concept here. Urban culture may be minimized and compromised in this model eldorado, but is shockingly authentically represented with all of the facets of a mass society: the crowds of people at the flea market under the subway viaduct, a police deployment at the soccer stadium, or groups of dancers on the trucks of the Love Parade. Lifelike arrangements present a big city life which is rocked by events. At most, the natural aspects of the landscape are romanticized—like the paper maché mountains of the reconstructed Alps. Nearby, the reinforced concrete skeleton of a new train station rises behind the ruin of an industrial-era building. Visitors can look into an old public pool which has been upgraded to an indoor water park. Transformation processes are part of the model.

Im Miniatur Wunderland Hamburg
At the Miniature Wonderland in
Hamburg

HAMBURG IM MINIATUR WUNDERLAND

Doch wie wirklichkeitsnah präsentiert man im Miniatur Wunderland das eigene, das Hamburger Stadtbild? Und welche Rolle spielen dabei die Bauten der Nachkriegsmoderne? An der nachgebildeten Köhlbrandbrücke befestigen politische Aktivisten gerade ihr Transparent „Rettet die Elefanten". Doch die Baudenkmäler der 1950er und 1960er Jahre sind im aktuellen Miniaturprospekt der Hansestadt kaum vertreten. Der Besucher erkennt den Michel, die Speicherstadt, die Hafencity mit Elbphilharmonie und den Hauptbahnhof – aber auf den City-Hof (1957, Rudolf Klophaus), der eigentlich am Rand der Gleise stehen müsste, wurde vorsorglich verzichtet.

HAMBURG IN THE MINIATURE WONDERLAND

But how close to reality is the Hamburg cityscape presented in the Miniature Wonderland? And what role do post-war modernist buildings play? On the reproduced Köhlbrand Bridge, political activists are hanging a handmade sign: "Save the Elephants." But the architectural monuments of the 1950s and 1960s are scarcely represented in the current miniature version of the Hanseatic city. Visitors will recognize the Michel, the Speicherstadt, the Hafencity with the Elbe Philharmonic Hall, and Hamburg Main Station—but the model builders have omitted the City-Hof (1957, Rudolf Klophaus), which should be located at the edge of the train tracks.

Am Bronzemodell der Hamburger
Innenstadt vor dem Rathaus
At the bronze model of Hamburg's
inner city in front of city hall

THE BRONZE MODEL IN FRONT OF CITY HALL

The city of Hamburg, which is the owner of the City-Hof, has cleared the complex for demolition, despite the fact that it is under monument protection and that it is in violation of its own laws. In order to experience the high-rise ensemble in miniature, one has to leave Miniature Wonderland and go out in the fresh air, ironically enough to the Senate side of city hall. At this location, there is a bronze model of the inner city, where the silhouette of the City-Hof will remain sculpturally perceptible, even in the future. The relief helps (seeing-impaired) people get a better idea of the height, distance and relationship between buildings. The prominent, nationwide debate about the preservation of the City-Hof was not able to stop the decision to demolish the ensemble. But in this model, the dispersed urban design of post-war modernism remains visually and tactilely perceptible.

THE CITY-HOF AT THE ARCHITECTURE ARCHIVE

It is certainly exciting to follow the changes to the cityscape at the Miniature Wonderland. But the model builders just cannot keep up with the pace of current developments; the changes to the city are happening too quickly. The need for tradition has definitely fallen by the wayside in Hamburg—in the case of the City-Hof, there is one exception which offers a little consolation. The original model from the construction period was donated to the Hamburg Architecture Archive. Now it waits to be restored—somehow a fitting commentary on the current situation. Nevertheless, after restoration it will be rid of the dust and patina of the intervening decades—in contrast to the neglected high-rise ensemble.

DAS BRONZEMODELL VOR DEM RATHAUS

Die Stadt Hamburg hat als Eigentümer trotz Denkmalschutz den City-Hof unter Missachtung der eigenen Gesetze zum Abriss freigegeben. Um das Hochhausensemble doch im kleinen Maßstab wahrnehmen zu können, muss man aus dem Miniatur Wunderland an die frische Luft wechseln. Ausgerechnet an die Senatsseite des Rathauses. Hier steht ein Bronzemodell der

Innenstadt und hier wird auch in Zukunft die Silhouette des City-Hofs plastisch erfassbar sein. Das Relief hilft (nicht allein) sehbehinderten Menschen, sich der Höhe, der Entfernung und dem Beziehungsgeflecht der Gebäude anzunähern. Die landesweite und prominent geführte Debatte um den Erhalt des City-Hofs hat den Abrissbeschluss nicht verhindern können. Doch mit diesem Modell bleibt der aufgelockerte Städtebau der Nachkriegsmoderne weiterhin sinnlich erlebbar.

DER CITY-HOF IM
ARCHITEKTURARCHIV

Die wirkliche Stadtbildveränderung
im Miniatur Wunderland zu verfolgen
hat ihren Reiz. Aber die Modellbauer
werden die momentane Entwicklung
wohl im Kleinen kaum so schnell
umsetzen können, wie sie im Großen
voranschreitet. Das Bedürfnis nach
Überlieferung bleibt in Hamburg
heute jedenfalls auf der Strecke – im
Fall des City-Hofs mit einer wenig
tröstlichen Ausnahme. Das Original-
modell aus der Erbauungszeit wurde
dem Hamburgischen Architekturarchiv überlassen. Nun wartet es auf
die Restaurierung, was als ange-
messener Kommentar zur aktuellen
Situation verstanden werden kann.
Allerdings wird es dann – im Gegen-
satz zum tatsächlich vernachlässig-
ten Hochhausensemble – den Staub
und die Patina der vergangenen
Jahrzehnte verlieren.

Mit Karl Heinz Hoffmann vom Ham-
burgischen Architekturarchiv am
Modell des City-Hofs
With Karl Heinz Hoffmann from the
Hamburg Architecture Archive by a
model of the City-Hof

MODELLE UND BAUTEN

MODELS AND BUILDINGS

MATTHIAS LUDWIG

Hochhaus

HIGH-RISE

MODELLBAUSATZ:
Hochhaus, 905
(ab 1965: B-905)

MODEL ASSEMBLY KIT:
High-rise, 905
(from 1965: B-905)

PRODUKTIONSZEITRAUM:
1958 bis 1987

PRODUCTION PERIOD:
1958 until 1987

HERSTELLER:
Gebr. Faller GmbH, Gütenbach
im Schwarzwald

MANUFACTURER:
Gebr. Faller GmbH, Gütenbach
in the Black Forest

MASSE:
15 x 10 x 28,7 cm

MEASUREMENTS:
15 x 10 x 28.7 cm

Als Mittelpunkt einer modernen (Teil-)Stadt sah man das Faller-Hochhaus wie selbstverständlich in den Modellbahnbüchern und -katalogen der 1960er bis 1980er Jahre. Dennoch scheint die Verbreitung eher begrenzt: Der Bausatz war relativ teuer und aufwendig zu bauen – und das 28,7 Zentimeter hohe Gebäude im H0-Maßstab brauchte viel Platz, um Wirkung zu entfalten. Aber auf ungezählten Wunschzetteln stand das Hochhaus ganz weit oben: Es sollte vom Mercedes-Stern bekrönt, von weiterer Moderne umgeben und Fallers Miniatur-Autobahn „ams" umfahren werden. Das reale Vorbild fand sich nicht im städtischen Umfeld. In Gütenbach im Schwarz-

The Faller high-rise was the natural centerpiece of a modern city (district) in model railway books and catalogs between the 1960s and the 1980s. However, the actual distribution of the model seems to be fairly limited: the assembly kit was relatively expensive and complicated to build—and the 28.7-centimeter-high building in H0 scale required a lot of space to unfold its full effect. However, the high-rise was at the top of countless wish lists. It was supposed to be crowned with a Mercedes star, surrounded by other modernist buildings, and be circumvented by Faller's miniature highway "ams." The building on which it was based was not located in an urban setting. The

wald hatten die Faller-Brüder in den späten 1950er Jahren begonnen, ihren Firmensitz mit urbaner Geste um Hochbauten für Verwaltung und Fabrikation (1959/63, Leopold Messmer) zu erweitern.

Im direkten Vergleich mit dem Modell offenbaren sich Ähnlichkeiten wie Abweichungen. Beide erheben sich auf einem rechteckigen Grundriss und zeigen ein überstehendes Flachdach mit einstöckigem Aufbau. Doch bietet das „kleine" Hochhaus fast doppelt so viele Etagen, eine andere Fassadenordnung und eine Ladenzone im Erdgeschoss. Grundsätzlich aber entspricht das Modell ebenso wie das Faller-Werk den westdeutschen Verwaltungshäusern jener Zeit. Ein stilistisch verwandtes Hochhaus findet sich etwa in Kassels Treppenstraße als Kopfbau (1955, Walter Seidel/Kurt Fleischmann). Ähnliches – mit symmetrischen Rasterfassaden und überstehenden Flach-, Krag- oder gar Flugdächern – steht in Nürnberg oder Köln, stand einst auch in Frankfurt am Main. Zunächst hatte Faller für die 1955 eingeführten „Stadtbausätze" eine moderne Erweiterung entwickelt, von der erste Bauplatten kurz darauf erhältlich waren. 1958 erschien dann

Faller brothers began to expand their company headquarters in Gütenbach in the Black Forest in 1950; with high-rises for administration and fabrication as an urban gesture (1959/63, Leopold Messmer). A direct comparison between these buildings and the model reveals similarities and differences. Both emerge from a rectangular foundation and have a protruding flat roof with a one-story superstructure. However, the "small" high-rise offers nearly twice as many stories, a different facade structure, and a

Der Faller-Firmensitz in Gütenbach im Schwarzwald im Katalog 1959/60 und heute
The Faller company headquarters in Gütenbach in the Black Forest in the 1959/60 catalog and today

Der Faller-Firmensitz in Gütenbach im Schwarzwald
The Faller company headquarters in Gütenbach in the Black Forest

loading zone on the ground floor. Nonetheless, similar to the Faller factory, the model fundamentally corresponds to the West German administrative buildings of the period. A stylistically related high-rise can be found on Treppenstraße in Kassel at the end of an ensemble (1955, Walter Seidel/Kurt Fleischmann). Similar buildings—with symmetrical grid-like facades and protruding flat, cantilever, or even floating roofs—are located in Nuremberg or Cologne, and were once also located in Frankfurt am Main.

In 1955, Faller introduced the "city assembly kits"; a modern extension for these kits was released a short time later. In 1958, a "special kit for the construction of a high-rise, which

unter der Nummer 905 ein „Speziel-
ler Satz für den Bau eines Hoch-
hauses, kann etwas abgewandelt
werden". Aus dem Bausatz entfaltete
man in den 1960er Jahren weitere
moderne Stadthäuser. Bis 1971
wurde das Hochhausmodell durch
Werbeschriftzüge und Reklame-
zeichen aufgewertet. Unter Zukauf
von Elektroteilen konnte man es um
eine etagenweise Beleuchtung, eine
Leuchtreklame und einen motorbe-
triebenen Drehstern ergänzen. Bald
aber sank der Stern von „B-905".
Nach und nach verabschiedete sich
Faller vom modernen Stadthaus, die
historische Ostzeile des Frankfurter
Römerbergs kam auf – und das
Hochhaus fiel 1987 endgültig aus
dem Programm.

can be adjusted somewhat" was
released under the number 905. This
assembly kit gave way to additional
modern urban buildings over the
course of the 1960s. Until 1971, the
high-rise model was upgraded with
lettered signs and logos. Through
the additional purchase of electrical
parts, one could light up individual
stories, add illuminated advertising,
or even a motor-powered turning
Mercedes star. However, soon the
"B-905" star waned. Little by little,
Faller took leave of the modernist
high-rise. The historical Ostzeile from
Frankfurt's Römerberg emerged—
and, in 1987, the high-rise was finally
discontinued.

DANIEL BARTETZKO

Villa im Tessin

VILLA IN TICINO

MODELLBAUSATZ:
Villa im Tessin, B-271 (bei der
ersten Wiederaufnahme: 1283)

PRODUKTIONSZEITRAUM:
1961 bis 1984, Wiederaufnah-
men (mit Unterbrechungen) bis
ca. 2000, seit 2016

HERSTELLER:
Gebr. Faller GmbH, Gütenbach
im Schwarzwald

MODEL ASSEMBLY KIT:
Villa in Ticino, B-271 (at the first
resumption: 1283)

PRODUCTION PERIOD:
1961 to 1984, resumptions (with
interruptions) until around 2000,
then since 2016

MANUFACTURER:
Gebr. Faller GmbH Gütenbach in
the Black Forest

Wohnen wie ein Hollywoodstar – in
der Schweiz. Alberto (*1930) und
Aldo Guscetti (*1931) machten es
möglich. Mit ihrem „Studio Tecnico"
in Ambrì am Südende des Gotthards
revolutionierten die Brüder vor 60
Jahren die Architektur der Region:
Sockelgeschosse in Bruchstein,
kastenförmige Obergeschosse,
riesige Fensterflächen und – Skan-
dal! – Flachdächer kennzeichneten
ihre Entwürfe. Mit gerade Mitte
zwanzig verwirklichten sie mehrere
solcher Bauten in der Leventina,
1958 auch eine Villa für ihren
Cousin Giovanni Guscetti an der
Hauptstraße ihres Heimatorts. Zwei
holzverkleidete Quader über einem
Bruchstein-Erdgeschoss, zwischen

Living like a Hollywood star—in Swit-
zerland. Alberto (*1930) and Aldo
Guscetti (*1931) made it possible.
With their "Studio Tecnico" in Ambrì
at the south end of the Gotthard, the
brothers revolutionized the architecture of the region in the 1960s: elevated basement levels of undressed
stone, box-shaped upper stories,
enormous window areas, and—how
scandalous—flat roofs characterized
their designs. In their mid-twenties,
the brothers had already realized several such buildings in the Leventina;
in 1958, they also constructed a villa
for their cousin, Giovanni Guscetti,
on the main street of their hometown.
Two wood-paneled cubes on top of
an undressed stone ground floor,

ihnen ein gemauerter Kamin und der kunstvoll verschobene Eingang, prägen ein Gebäude, das wie ein gelandetes UFO in der traditionellen Bergdorf-Umgebung gewirkt haben muss. Der Geist von Frank Lloyd Wright wehte durchs Tessin.

Wer aus Deutschland in den Süden wollte, fuhr durch Ambrì. So auch der Spielzeugproduzent Hermann Faller. Auf dem Weg zu seinem Ferienhaus am Lago Maggiore passierte er das Guscetti-Kunstwerk. Und es entstand sein Wunsch, selbst ein solches Haus zu bewohnen. Den Plan verwirklichte der Häuslebauer doppelt. Im Faller-Werk schuf der Modell-Entwickler Oswald Scherzinger den Kunststoff-Bausatz des Schweizer Vorbilds. Und der junge Firmenarchitekt Leopold Messmer entwarf zeitgleich eine schnittige Villa, die alle wesentlichen Merkmale des Guscetti-Baus aufwies. Seit 1961 thront sie am Hang über Gütenbach: ein Traumhaus und ein Statement. Das UFO war im Schwarzwald gelandet.

Keins der deutschen Häuser ist eine exakte Kopie. Der Plastik-Miniatur setzte man quergerichtete, grandios sinnfreie Schmetterlingsdächer auf. Ihre Obergeschosse sind verdreht,

in between a stone fireplace and an artistically displaced entryway characterize the building, which must have seemed like a landed UFO in the traditional mountain village surroundings. The ghost of Frank Lloyd Wright blew through Ticino.

Anyone who wanted to travel south from Germany had to drive through Ambrì. This was also the case for model manufacturer Hermann Faller. He passed the Guscetti work of art on the way to his vacation home on Lago Maggiore. And thus arose the desire to live in a house like that himself, a plan which he realized twice. The model developer Oswald Scherzinger created a plastic assembly kit modelled on the Swiss villa at the Faller factory. And the young company architect, Leopold Messmer, simultaneously designed a stylish villa that boasted all the key characteristics of the Guscetti building. Since 1961, the villa has been sitting high up on a hillside over Gütenbach: a dream house and a statement. The UFO had landed in the Black Forest.

None of the German houses are an exact copy. Grandiose and pointless crosswise butterfly roofs were added to the plastic miniature. Its upper

Die Villa Giovanni Guscetti in Ambrì im Tessin um 1958 und heute
The villa Giovanni Guscetti in Ambrì in Ticino around 1958 and today

Die Villa Giovanni Guscetti in Ambrì
im Tessin
The villa Giovanni Guscetti in Ambrì
in Ticino

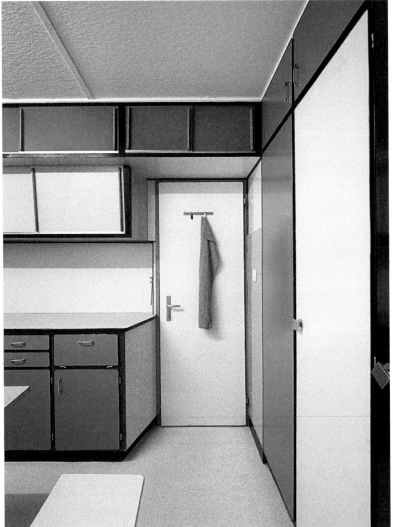

LINKS Die Villa Giovanni Guscetti in
Ambrì im Tessin
LEFT The villa Giovanni Guscetti in
Ambrì in Ticino

OBEN Die Villa Hermann Faller in
Gütenbach im Schwarzwald
ABOVE The Hermann Faller villa in
Gütenbach in the Black Forest

vorbildgetreue Details finden sich an anderen Stellen wieder. Die „große" Villa, die Hermann Faller in Gütenbach bis 1982 bewohnte, variiert den Urbau weiter: Die von parallelen Flugdächern bekrönten Obergeschosse sind Richtung Tal gedreht. Seitlich angeschlossen befand sich ein (mittlerweile abgerissenes) Schwimmbad. Mehrfach begegnen dem Betrachter bizarr gerasterte Gitter, die man von Faller-Häusern kennt – den Modellbahnhäusern! In den 1960ern gingen die Guscetti-Brüder im Tessin getrennte Wege. Sie erfuhren Jahre später vom vermeintlichen Plagiat. Verübelt haben sie es nicht: Das Modell sei recht unterschiedlich zu ihrem Haus, sagten sie 2016 in einem Interview im Schweizer Fernsehen und billigten den von ihnen inspirierten Bauten und Bauherrn „maximale Freiheit" zu. Immerhin nannte Faller den über 40 Jahre lang produzierten Bausatz im Katalog stets korrekt „Villa im Tessin".

stories are distorted; other aspects correspond to the original. The "big" villa in Gütenbach, in which Hermann Faller lived until 1982, made additional changes to the original on which it was based. The upper levels, which are parallel and crowned with floating roofs, are turned in the direction of the valley. On the side there was an attached pool (which has since been demolished). In multiple places, the observer is met by the bizarrely rastered fences which are typical of Faller buildings—the model train houses! In the 1960s, the Guscetti brothers went separate ways in Ticino. Years later they learned of the alleged plagiarism. But they did not resent it: they said in a 2016 interview on Swiss television that the model was very different from their house and granted "maximum freedom" to the buildings and builders that they had inspired. At least Faller always described the assembly kit, which was produced for 40 years, correctly as the "Villa in Ticino."

Die Villa Hermann Faller in Gütenbach im Schwarzwald
The Hermann Faller villa in Gütenbach in the Black Forest

VERENA PFEIFFER-KLOSS

Auto-Rast

REST STOP

MODELLBAUSATZ:
Auto-Rast mit Tanksäulen und
Restaurant, B-214 (mit Motor:
B-215); Snack-Bar, B-137

PRODUKTIONSZEITRAUM:
1961 bis 1965 (B-214); 1961 bis
1972/73 (B-215); 1975 bis 1980
(B-137)

HERSTELLER:
Gebr. Faller GmbH, Gütenbach
im Schwarzwald

MASSE:
12 x 9 x 9 cm (B-214/215);
12 x 8 x 10 cm (B-137)

MODEL ASSEMBLY KIT:
Rest stop with petrol pumps and
a restaurant, B-214 (with motor:
B-215); snack bar, B-137

PRODUCTION PERIOD:
1961 to 1965 (B-214); 1961 to
1972/73 (B-215); 1975 to 1980
(B-137)

MANUFACTURER:
Gebr. Faller GmbH, Gütenbach in
the Black Forest

MEASUREMENTS:
12 x 9 x 9 cm (B-214/215);
12 x 8 x 10 cm (B-137)

Auto, Ausflug, Auftanken: Mit dem
Modell B-214/215, einer Tankstelle
mit aufgesetztem Rundrestaurant
und Mercedes-Stern, inszenierte
Faller ab 1961 die Autofahrt als Frei-
zeiterlebnis. Das Tanken wurde mit
dem freien Blick auf das Verkehrsge-
schehen bei Essen und Trinken verbunden. In einem runden Wintergar-
ten mit umlaufendem Balkon thront
das Restaurant über drei gelb-roten
Zapfsäulen. Hinter diesen (sie waren
ebenso mit dem Modell B-217
„Shell-Tankstelle ODZ 1" erhältlich)
findet sich das Kassenhäuschen,
an das sich die geschwungenen
Auflager des Obergeschosses und
die rote Zugangstreppe schmiegen.
Bekrönt wird das Restaurantdach

Car, day trip, fueling up: from 1961
onward, Faller incorporated driving
as a pastime through the model
B-214/215, a gas station with a
restaurant on the second floor and a
Mercedes star. Fueling up was combined with eating and drinking while
enjoying a clear view of the busy
street. The round conservatory with
its circumferential balcony houses
a restaurant which perches above
three yellow and red fuel pumps.
Behind the pumps (they were also
available in the model B-217 "Shell
gas station ODZ 1") is the atten-
dant's booth, on which the curved
supports for the upper story and the
red access stairs are nestled. For
an additional charge, the roof of the

Das Autohaus „Breisgau" in Freiburg im Breisgau in den frühen 1950er Jahren und in seiner heutigen Restaurant-Nutzung
The service station "Breisgau" in Freiburg im Breisgau in the early 1950s and today, in its current use as a restaurant

von dem gegen Aufpreis elektrisch drehbaren Mercedes-Stern, der ein Zeichen moderner Mobilität in die Modellanlage setzt. Dieser konnte je nach Belieben durch mitgelieferte Signets von VW, Opel oder Ford ersetzt werden. Nach kurzer Unterbrechung wurde das Modell in den späten 1970er Jahren ohne Zapfsäulen und Drehlogo als „Snack-Bar" angeboten.

Das zehn Jahre ältere Vorbild, das zweigeschossige sogenannte Turmcafé mit Tankstelle in Freiburg-Zähringen, wurde 1951 nach Plänen von Wilhelm (Willi) Schelkes (1904–1999) errichtet. Schelkes war bis Kriegsende im Büro Albert Speer, danach als freier Architekt in Freiburg tätig. Sein Turmcafé gehörte damals zum Opel-Haus „Breisgau". Der weiße Bau besteht aus einem zweigeschossigen Turm auf zwölfeckigem Grundriss mit großen Fensterflächen und trägt ein schlankes, rechtwinkliges Vordach, das weit über die Zapfsäulen ragt. Über eine gewendelte, freistehende Außentreppe aus Sichtbeton wird das Obergeschoss erreicht. Offenheit, Sachlichkeit und klare Formen prägen diesen Bau, der mit großer Geste zur freien Fahrt aufruft. Derzeit

restaurant could be crowned by an electrically rotating Mercedes logo, which gave the model a clear sign of modern mobility. The Mercedes star could be replaced by those of VW, Opel, or Ford, which were included. After a short interruption in production, the model was offered in the 1970s without fuel pumps and rotating logo as a "snack bar."

The building on which the model is based, the two-story so-called "tower cafe" with a gas station in Freiburg-Zähringen, is ten years older. The original building was constructed in 1951 following plans by Wilhelm (Willi) Schelkes (1904–1999). Schelkes worked in Albert Speer's office until the end of the war; afterwards, he worked as a freelance architect in Freiburg. Back then, his tower cafe was part of the Opel dealership "Breisgau." The white building is made up of a two-story, twelve-sided tower with large windows and a slim, rectangular canopy which extends well beyond the fuel pumps. The upper story is reached via a free-standing spiral staircase made of exposed concrete. The building is characterized by openness, practicality, and clear forms; with its generous gesture,

Das sogenannte Turmcafé in Freiburg im Breisgau während einer Ausstellung der Braunschweiger Künstlerin Christina Kersten und im städtebaulichen Umfeld
The so-called Turmcafé in Freiburg im Breisgau during an exhibition by the Braunschweig artist Christina Kersten and in the urban context

dient die Anlage nach denkmalgerechter Sanierung – inzwischen von Wohnbauten umringt – als Biergarten, Ausstellungs- und Veranstaltungsraum eines Restaurants.
Trotz der funktionalen Verwandtschaft unterscheiden sich Vorbild und Bausatz grundlegend. Die bunte, runde, geschlossene Architektur des Modells vermittelt beinahe biedere Gemütlichkeit. Es ist mehr Kirmes als Bauhaus, mehr Ankunft

it sings the song of the open road. Following a historically appropriate renovation, the building—which is meanwhile surrounded by housing—now serves as a beer garden and as the exhibition and event space for a restaurant.
Despite the functional relationship, the assembly kit and the building are fundamentally different. The colorful, round, closed architecture of the model conveys almost conservative

als Abfahrt. Diese freie Interpretation nachkriegsmoderner Tankstellen und Ausflugslokale spiegelt die Wünsche und Widersprüche des damaligen mobilen Lebensgefühls. Vielleicht ist auch daher die „Auto-Rast" ein so langjährig verkauftes Faller-Modell. Sein Stern dreht sich bis heute in zahlreichen Modellbahnlandschaften, dank des robusten Bürstenmotors.

comfort. It is more carnival than Bauhaus, more arrival than departure. This free interpretation of post-war modernist gas stations and destination restaurants reflects the desires and the contradictions of the mobile lifestyle of the time. Maybe that is the reason why the Faller model "Rest stop" has been sold for so many years. Its star still rotates over countless model train sets, owing to the robust brush motor.

KARIN BERKEMANN

Moderne Kirche

MODERN CHURCH

MODELLBAUSATZ:
Moderne Kirche, B-235

PRODUKTIONSZEITRAUM:
1965 bis 1980

HERSTELLER:
Gebr. Faller GmbH, Gütenbach
im Schwarzwald

MASSE:
14 x 14 x 17,7 cm

MODEL ASSEMBLY KIT:
Modern church, B-235

PRODUCTION PERIOD:
1965 until 1980

MANUFACTURER:
Gebr. Faller GmbH, Gütenbach in
the Black Forest

MEASUREMENTS:
14 x 14 x 17.7 cm

Die transparente Front, das überstrahlte Kreuz und die überaus zeichenhaften Dachfenster – all das wirkt fast wie eine freigeistig-amerikanische Drive-In-Church. Doch im Faller-Katalog von 1965 findet sich unser Modell „Moderne Kirche" direkt neben einem Miniatur-Geistlichen, den seine Kleidung klar als evangelisch kennzeichnet. Und produziert wurde der Bausatz von zwei Brüdern altkatholischen Glaubens. Hermann und Edwin Faller verkauften schon früh und mit großer Selbstverständlichkeit ihre Kleinkirchen und Bergkapellen als „immer dankbare Modelle". 1965 klang der Begleittext plötzlich verhalten: „Auch in unserer Zeit ist die Kirche als dominierender

The transparent front, the lit-up cross, and the extremely symbolic skylight—these aspects make this church seem almost like a free-spirited American drive-in church. But this model, "Modern church," appears in the 1965 Faller catalog next to a miniature pastor whose clothing clearly identify him as a Protestant. This assembly kit was produced by two brothers of Old Catholic faith. Hermann and Edwin Faller began selling small churches and mountain chapels early on; they regarded this as quite natural and described the models as "always rewarding." In 1965, the accompanying text was suddenly cautious: "even today, the fact that the church is the domi-

Mittelpunkt des Dorfes nicht hinweg zu denken." In diesem Umbruchsjahr brachte die „Moderne Kirche" einen neuen Stil und einen Hauch von Urbanität ins Sortiment: Das Modell sei „für Stadt oder Dorf geeignet". Das große Vorbild ist ausgerechnet eine römisch-katholische Kirche: St. Katharina überragt seit 1965 das ländliche Gütenbach, den Heimatort der Faller-Werke. Geplant wurde der Gottesdienstraum vom Erzbischöflichen Bauamt Freiburg (Oberbauamtmann Lothar Schmitt). Die Nähe zum Modell ist offenkundig: die hohe Straßenfront, der T-förmige Grundriss, das tiefe Satteldach, der kantige Glockenträger an der Seite. Doch, und damit fangen die Unterschiede an, er steht an der „falschen" Seite. Auch die prägenden Betongläser des Freiburger Künstlers Rainer Dorwarth (1924–2015) fehlen am Bausatz. Immerhin ließen sich die Plastikfenster mit den beigelegten Nassschieber-Bildchen aufhübschen. Es gab sogar eine Klebevorlage für einen Altar, der auf drei Stufen an die Wand gerückt wurde.

Damit zeigt die kleine Kirche einen Zwischenzustand der großen: Auf ersten Entwürfen soll der Turm von St. Katharina noch auf derselben

nant focus of the village cannot be denied." In this year of transition, the "Modern church" brought a new style and a touch of urbanity into the production line: the model was "suitable for cities or villages."

The building on which the model was based is ironically a Roman Catholic church: since 1965, St. Katharina towers over rural Gütenbach, the home of the Faller factory. The church was designed by the building authorities of the archdiocese Freiburg (senior site engineer Lothar Schmitt). The closeness to the model is obvious: the high street front, the T-shaped floor plan, the deep pitched roof, the angular bell tower on the side. However, and this is where the differences begin, the bell tower is on the "wrong" side. And the characteristic glass pavers by the Freiburg artist Rainer Dorwarth (1924–2015) are also missing from the assembly kit. At least the plastic windows could be dressed up with the transfers included with the set. There was even a gluing template for an altar, which was placed against the wall on three steps.

In this respect, the small church represents an intermediate state of planning of the big one: in the initial

St. Katharina in Gütenbach im
Schwarzwald während des Baus
um 1964 und heute
St. Katharina in Gütenbach in the
Black Forest during construction
around 1964 and today

St. Katharina in Gütenbach im
Schwarzwald heute
St. Katharina in Gütenbach in
the Black Forest today

Seite gestanden haben wie beim Modell. Auch kamen die „echten" Betonglasfenster erst hinzu, als der Faller-Bausatz schon längst produktionsfertig sein musste. Und nicht zuletzt spiegelte der Miniatur-Klebe-Altar noch die Messfeier vor den Reformen des Zweiten Vatikanischen Konzils (1962–1965) – in St. Katharina gab es zunächst ein hölzernes Provisorium, später eine künstlerisch-liturgische Neuordnung. Die Modellbauwelt ermöglichte so 1965 eine konfessionelle Mischung, die in

designs, the tower of St. Katharina was supposed to be on the same side as the model's. The "real" glass pavers were also added after the Faller assembly kit was likely already ready for production. And, last but not least, the miniature altar which is glued in place reflects the celebration of mass from before the reforms of the Second Vatican Council (1962–1965)—in St. Katharina there was first a temporary wooden altar, then later an artistic and liturgical restructuring. In 1965, the model

RECHTS Der Altarraum von St. Katharina in Gütenbach um 1978 vor der liturgischen Neuordnung und ein Blick ins Innere des Faller-Kirchenmodells
RIGHT The chancel of St. Katharina in Gütenbach around 1978 before the liturgical restructuring and a view into the interior of the Faller church model

LINKS St. Katharina in Gütenbach im Schwarzwald heute
LEFT St. Katharina in Gütenbach in the Black Forest today

der Wirklichkeit damals hätte scheitern müssen. Vielleicht war es eine feine Blüte ökumenischen Humors. Vielleicht war es die Aufbruchsstimmung jener bewegten Jahre. In jedem Fall machte auch und gerade diese Offenheit die Faller-Kirche zu einer modernen.

world made a denominational mix possible that would have failed in reality. Maybe it was a fine example of ecumenical humor. Maybe it was the optimistic mood of those eventful years. In any case, it was this openness above all which made the Faller church a modern one.

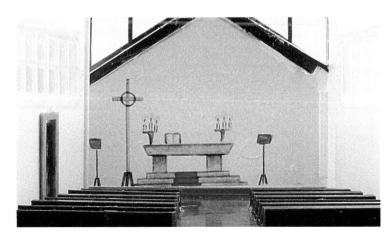

C. JULIUS REINSBERG

Bahnhof „Neustadt"

TRAIN STATION "NEUSTADT"

MODELLBAUSATZ:
Bahnhof „Neustadt", B-111

PRODUKTIONSZEITRAUM:
1966 bis 1983, seit 2016

HERSTELLER:
Gebr. Faller GmbH, Gütenbach
im Schwarzwald

MASSE:
52,9 x 15,8 x 9,8 cm

MODEL ASSEMBLY KIT:
Train station "Neustadt", B-111

PRODUCTION PERIOD:
1966 until 1983, since 2016

MANUFACTURER:
Gebr. Faller GmbH, Gütenbach in
the Black Forest

MEASUREMENTS:
52.9 x 15.8 x 9.8 cm

„Neustadt", man kann sich keinen passenderen Namen für die deutsche Durchschnittsstadt vorstellen: regional nicht festgeschrieben, dem Status als Dorf entwachsen, aber meist mit einer überschaubaren Einwohnerzahl. Neustadt an der Weinstraße bildet mit gut 50.000 Einwohnern bereits den Ausreißer nach oben. Es verwundert also nicht, dass sich der Schriftzug „Neustadt" ab 1966 auch auf dem Faller-Bahnhofsbausatz wiederfindet. Für ein Städtchen auf der Modellplatte wirkt er unabhängig von dessen konkreter Gestalt sofort schlüssig. Der entsprechende Bausatz dagegen scheint zunächst gar nicht in die Welt der Halbprovinz zu passen. Der

"Neustadt." It is scarcely possible to find a more fitting name for the average German town. Not regionally specific, larger than a village, but usually with a modest number of residents. Neustadt an der Weinstraße is already at the upper end of the scale with circa 50,000 residents. It is therefore unsurprising that the lettering "Neustadt" can also be found from 1966 onward on the Faller train station assembly kit. It seems immediately logical for the little town on the model board, regardless of its concrete design. The respective assembly kit, on the other hand, seems at first not to fit at all into the world of the mid-sized town. Is the archetype of the "Neustadt" train station really

Archetyp des „Neustädter" Bahnhofs – ein eleganter, flachgedeckter Klinkerbau mit herausgehobener Schalterhalle?

Das reale Vorbild steht in keinem der zahlreichen Orte namens Neustadt, sondern in der Stadt Goch am Niederrhein. Mit einer Einwohnerzahl zwischen 15.000 und 20.000 entsprach sie in den 1950er Jahren der beschriebenen Kleinstadtnorm. Der Bahnhof zeigt sich dagegen alles andere als provinziell. Dieser geradezu großstädtisch anmutende Bau wurde 1957 vom Klever Architekten Toni Hermanns (1915–2007) errichtet, der kurz darauf mit der Duisburger Liebfrauenkirche reüssieren sollte. Der beherrschende Mitteltrakt beherbergt die Empfangshalle und somit das funktionale Herzstück der Anlage. Ihre breite, in Richtung Stadt blickende Fensterfront wird durch ein Raster aus hochrechteckigen Stahlprofilen untergliedert. Rechts und links wird sie von zwei vertikalen Klinkerwänden eingefasst, die vom Bahnsteig zum Bahnhofsvorplatz hin dynamisch emporstreben. An die Halle schließt eine einstöckige, flachgedeckte Bebauung an, die Bürotrakt und Bahnhofsgaststätte mit Pächterwohnung aufnimmt.

an elegant brick building with a flat roof and an accentuated main hall? The real building on which the model was based is not located in one of the numerous Neustadts in Germany, but rather in the town of Goch on the Lower Rhine. With a population between 15,000 and 20,000, Goch conformed to the small town norm of the 1950s. The train station on the other hand was anything but provincial. This almost metropolitan-seeming building was built by the architect Toni Hermanns (1915–2007) from Kleve, who shortly after had great success with the Liebfrauenkirche in Duisburg. The dominant central section contains the arrival hall and thus the functional heart of the building. Its wide window front faces the town and is subdivided by a grid of upright rectangular steel profiles. It is framed left and right by two vertical brick walls, which dynamically strive upwards from the track to the station square. A one-story building with a flat roof is attached to the hall that contains offices, the station restaurant, and the superintendents' apartment. As it happens, the building is archetypal in several ways. The design, which seems a bit oversized for the

Das Faller-Modell „Bahnhof ‚Neustadt'" in den 1960er Jahren vor seinem Vorbild, dem Bahnhof im niederrheinischen Goch, und das Bahnhofsgebäude heute
The Faller model "Train station 'Neustadt'" in the 1960s in front of the building it was modeled on, the Lower Rhine town of Goch and the train station today

Das Bahnhofsgebäude in Goch heute
The Goch train station today

Tatsächlich ist das Bauwerk in mehrfacher Hinsicht archetypisch. Die gestalterische Geste, die für die Kleinstadt etwas überdimensioniert wirkt, versinnbildlicht die – oft uneingelösten – Fortschrittsversprechen und Wachstumsprognosen der Wirtschaftswunderjahre. Die offene, lichtdurchflutete Architektur wirkt dabei wie ein Vorbote: In manchen bundesdeutschen Großstädten der 1950er gehörten entsprechende Bahnhofsbauten bereits unauflöslich zur urbanen Identität, etwa in Köln oder Würzburg. Die Umwandlung zum Modellbausatz erfolgte ungewöhnlich detailgetreu, bis hin zur exakten Nachbildung des Haupteingangs mit Glasbausteinmuster, vorkragendem Dach und asymmetrisch aufgepflanzter Runduhr. Als Klassiker erlebte das Modell 2016 eine Wiederauflage.

small town, epitomized the—often unfulfilled—promise of progress and predictions of growth during the economic wonder years. The open architecture is flooded with light and feels like a forerunner. In the 1950s, these types of train buildings were an integral part of the urban identity of West German cities such as Cologne or Würzburg. The transformation to a model took place with an unusual degree of accuracy, including the exact reproduction of the main entrance with its glass brick pattern, projecting roof, and asymmetrically placed clock. The model was reintroduced as a classic in 2016.

RALF LIPTAU

Postamt Badenweiler

BADENWEILER POST OFFICE

MODELLBAUSATZ:
Postamt Badenweiler, B-8150

PRODUKTIONSZEITRAUM:
1970 bis um 1990

HERSTELLER:
Kibri (Kindler & Briel GmbH),
Böblingen

MASSE:
24 x 20 x 9 cm

MODEL ASSEMBLY KIT:
Badenweiler post office, B-8150

PRODUCTION PERIOD:
1970 until about 1990

MANUFACTURER:
Kibri (Kindler & Briel GmbH),
Böblingen

MEASUREMENTS:
24 x 20 x 9 cm

Das „Postamt Badenweiler", das aus Plastik: Es schwebt. Der weitgehend transparente Hauptteil ruht auf einem zurückgenommenen Sockel, der durch seinen dunklen Anstrich beinahe verschwindet. Wie eine angedockte Gangway bildet die Zugangstreppe scheinbar die einzige Verbindung zur Straße. Vorgeführt wird uns eine reduzierte Crownhall (1956, Ludwig Mies van der Rohe), die scheinbar von Chicago aus zum Landeanflug auf der Modellbahnplatte ansetzt – und sich dann doch nicht recht dazu entschließen kann. Deshalb wird der Hauptbau umklammert von einem quergerichteten Zweigeschosser, der über den gläsernen Riegel greift. Zwar mit

The "Badenweiler post office" made of plastic seems to float. The extensively transparent main section sits on a recessed foundation which nearly disappears owing to a coat of dark paint. The access stairs appear to be the only connection to the street and feel like a gangway. We are presented with a reduced Crownhall (1956, Ludwig Mies van der Rohe) which has apparently been scheduled for arrival from Chicago—but still has not quite decided that it is going to land. For this reason, the main building is embraced by a crosswise two-story section which overlaps its glass mid-section. This section may have a modern flat roof, but is otherwise rather tamely

modernem Flachdach, aber sonst schön brav mit Balkon und Geranienkästen, verankert er das Postamt in der inszenierten süddeutschen Kleinstadtidylle. Entsprechend enthält der Bausatz auch eine Fundamenterweiterung, welche die Schauseite ergänzt und weiteren Blumenschmuck davor ermöglicht. Werbeschilder zum Aufkleben und ein Schriftzug fürs Dach tun ein Übriges, um die strenge Geometrie zu verunklären.

Ähnliches zeigt der Blick auf das wirkliche Postamt Badenweiler, das große aus Beton und Glas. In den Jahren 1962/63 gestaltete es der Freiburger Oberpostbaurat Hans Merkenthaler (1904–1968), der verbunden war mit der bayerischen Postbauschule und der Stuttgarter Schule um Bonatz und Schmitthenner. In Badenweiler formte Merkenthaler, noch gesteigert durch die Hanglage des Grundstücks, das Bild zweier ineinandergeschobener, über dem Boden schwebender Quader. Und auch die klare leichte Formensprache lässt das große Postamt „modellhaft" wirken. Als könne es ein Riese jederzeit verschieben oder wegnehmen. Doch das Alltägliche stört wieder die „reine" Konzeption: Hecken und Autos vor dem Bau

outfitted with a balcony and a flower box full of geraniums, and thus firmly anchored in the staged southern German small town idyll. The assembly kit also contains a foundation extension with which the model builder can add more flowers to the front side of the building. Advertising and lettering for the roof help to further obscure the strict geometry.

A look to the real Badenweiler post office, the one of concrete and glass, shows something similar. The post office was designed by Freiburg Oberpostbaurat [postal building commissioner] Hans Merkenthaler (1904–1968) in 1962/63; Merkenthaler was connected to the Bavarian school of post office construction and the Stuttgart school centered on Bonatz and Schmitthenner. In Badenweiler, Merkenthaler formed the image of two intersecting floating cuboids; this impression was enhanced by the location of the construction site at the top of a hill. The clear, light design of the large post office also makes it seem "model-like." As if a giant could come along at any moment and move it or take it away. However, day-to-day life disturbs the "pure" conception: hedges and cars in front of the

OBEN/FOLGEND Das Postamt in Badenweiler in den 1960er Jahren und heute
ABOVE/FOLLOWING The post office in Badenweiler in the 1960s and today

verdecken den Sockel. Werbeschilder – und immerhin auch noch ein Briefkasten – stehen vor dem Postamt oder sind an ihm angebracht. Abgesehen davon, dass der Bausatz dem realen Vorbild formal sehr nahekommt, hat also auch Kibri sein Plastik-Postamt in die kleinstädtische Lebenswelt eingebunden und an der Wirklichkeit entwickelt. Das Modell des Postamts funktioniert deshalb ganz anders, als es wohl bei einer zeitgenössischen Fotografie des Gebäudes wäre: Dem damaligen Geschmack folgend, hätte dort eine Retusche alle „störenden" Elemente entfernen müssen. Beim Bausatz geht es – bei aller Nähe zum Postamt aus Beton und Glas – aber nicht darum, architektonische Bilder zu wiederholen. Wichtig ist vielmehr die alltägliche Wirklichkeit der Bauten im Gebrauch.

building conceal the foundation. Advertisements—and of course a mailbox—are mounted in front of or on the building itself.

Independent of the fact that the model is formally very close to the real building on which it is based, Kibri also seemed to incorporate its plastic post office into the daily life of the small town and tried to develop it in a way that reflected reality. The model of the post office therefore functions quite differently to contemporary photos of the building. Following the taste of the time, the photo was retouched to remove all "distracting" elements. However, for the model—with all its similarity to the building of concrete and glass—it was not about repeating architectural photographs. It was much more about reproducing the daily reality of the buildings in use.

TERESA FANKHÄNEL

Wohnhausgruppe

GROUP OF APARTMENT BUILDINGS

MODELLBAUSATZ: Wohnhausgruppe, B 5730/129/633 (B 5457370/129/633, B 54 57370/129/00633); Hochhaus, B 5730/129/634 (B 5457370/129/634, B 5457370/129/00634)

PRODUKTIONSZEITRAUM: 1971 bis um 1990

HERSTELLER: VEB Kombinat Holzspielwaren VERO (Vereinigte Olbernhauer Spielwarenbetriebe), Olbernhau im Erzgebirge (ab 1980/81 Teil von: VEB Kombinat Spielwaren Sonneberg)

MASSE: 15 x 15 x 13,5 cm; 10,5 x 9,5 x 12,5 cm

MODEL ASSEMBLY KIT: Group of apartment buildings, B 5730/129/633 (B 5457370/129/633, B 5457370/129/00633); High-rise, B 5730/129/634 (B 5457370/129/634, B 5457370/129/00634)

PRODUCTION PERIOD: 1971 until around 1990

MANUFACTURER: VEB Kombinat Holzspielwaren VERO (Vereinigte Olbernhauer Spielwarenbetriebe), Olbernhau in the Ore Mountains (from 1980/81 part of VEB Kombinat Spielwaren Sonneberg)

MEASUREMENTS: 15 x 15 x 13.5 cm; 10.5 x 9.5 x 12.5 cm

Die Modelle „Wohnhausgruppe" und „Hochhaus" wurden auf der Leipziger Frühjahrsmesse 1971 erstmals der Öffentlichkeit präsentiert. Kurz zuvor hatte Vero beschlossen, auf Kunststoff umzustellen. Die farbenfrohen Module konnten zu Hochhäusern unterschiedlicher Höhe zusammengesetzt werden und bezogen sich auf „moderne Typen". Sie gingen dem wohl berühmtesten Plattenbau, dem WBS 70, um zwei Jahre voraus und griffen auf frühere Lösungen im Fertigbau zurück. Obwohl es kein konkretes Vorbild zu geben scheint, erinnern die Modelle an allgegenwärtige Elemente an damaligen ostdeutschen Wohnhäusern: auffällige Stützen im Erdgeschoss, neoklassi-

The models "Group of apartment buildings" and "High-rise" were first presented to the public at the Leipzig spring congress in 1971. Shortly before this point, Vero had decided to switch to plastic. The colorful modules could be combined into high-rises of varying heights and were based on "modern types." They preceded the most well-known slab construction type, the WBS 70, by two years and drew on earlier solutions for prefabrication. Despite the fact that there does not seem to be a concrete building on which the models were based, they remind the viewer of the ubiquitous elements of East German housing of the period: obvious supports on the ground

LINKS Die Erfurter PH16-Hochhäuser am Juri-Gagarin-Ring auf einer Post-karte der frühen 1970er Jahre
LEFT The Erfurt PH16 high-rises on Juri Gagarin Ring on a postcard from the early 1970s

RECHTS Sanierte PH16-Häuser in Erfurt am Juri-Gagarin-Ring
RIGHT Restored PH16 buildings in Erfurt on Juri Gagarin Ring

zistische Dächer und Dachterrassen, wie man sie am Pirnaischen Platz in Dresden, in der Siedlung Jena-Nord oder an den PH16-Häusern in Erfurt finden kann.

Modellbauhersteller schufen gerne fiktive Umgebungen für ihre Gebäude, die auf reale Orte anspielten. So wurde beispielsweise der Vero-Bahnhof „Thornstadt", ein Verweis auf die polnische Stadt Torun, in Verbindung mit dem Bausatz „Wohnhausgruppe" inszeniert. Ungeachtet des Namens war das Modell eine Anspielung auf bekannte Berliner S-Bahnhöfe wie

floor and neoclassical roofs and roof terraces. These elements can for example be seen at Pirnaischen Platz in Dresden, on the housing estate Jena-Nord, or in the PH16 buildings in Erfurt.

Model manufacturers liked to create fictional environments for their buildings which hinted at real locations. For example, the Vero train station "Thornstadt," which was displayed together with the assembly kit "Group of apartment buildings," referred to the Polish town Torun. Despite the name, the model was

am Alexanderplatz. In Torun gab es tatsächlich nie ein solches Gebäude. Auf gleiche Weise montierte man die Wohnhausgruppe für den Katalog in ein Foto des Leipziger Sachsenplatzes mit seinem modernen Informationszentrum (1969, Horst Krantz). Ebenso wurden die Bausätze in einem Werbe-Diorama zur Stadtlandschaft arrangiert, welche die wachsenden Großsiedlungen der Ostmoderne widerspiegelte.

Typologien und modulare Systeme waren dazu gedacht, das industrielle Bauen schneller und flexibler zu

actually an allusion to well-known Berlin S-bahn stations such as Alexanderplatz. There was never actually a building like this one in Torun. In the same way, the group of apartment buildings was mounted in front of a photo of Sachsenplatz in Leipzig, with its modern information center (1969, Horst Krantz), for the catalog. The models were also arranged in an advertising diorama that reflected the growing East German modernist housing estates.

Typologies and modular systems were put in place to make industrial

OBEN Vero-Hochhausmodelle auf
einem Diorama gruppiert zur ostmodernen Großsiedlung
ABOVE The Vero high-rise model in a
diorama grouped to create an East
German modernist housing estate

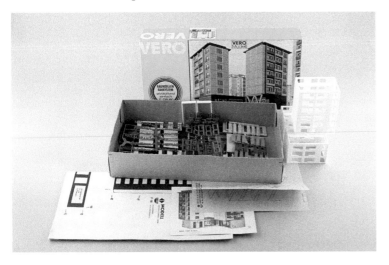

machine. Im kleinen Maßstab erleich-
terten die Module im Vero-„Raumzellen"-System eine rasche Montage.
Zugleich sollten die Modelle so für
mehrere Spurweiten nutzbar sein.
Das Erdgeschoss war deshalb in H0
gestaltet, während die Obergeschosse sich dem Maßstab TT annäherten.
Wie bei realen Architekturen konnten
die Elemente zu Gebäuden zusammengesetzt werden, die vom eher
bescheidenen Hochhaus auf dem
Schachtel-Cover abwichen. (Vero
nutzte diese Freiheit und bot auch
eine Minol-Tankstelle in der Form
des Hochhaus-Erdgeschosses an.)
Verglichen mit dem Kinderspiel „Der
kleine Großblock-Baumeister", das
von „plapsi" ab 1970 produziert und
aus Einzelteilen zusammengesetzt
wurde, waren die beiden Vero-Mo-
delle jedoch eher unflexibel: Jedes
Raumzellen-Modul umfasste in der
Regel drei Etagen, die Modellhöhe
blieb also auf ein Mehrfaches der
Zahl Drei beschränkt.

construction faster and more flexible.
On a small scale, the modules of the
Vero "compartment" system made
quick construction possible. At the
same time, the models were also
intended to be used for a variety of
track gauges. For this reason, the
ground floor was designed on an H0
scale, while the upper stories came
closer to a TT scale. Similar to their
real counterparts, the elements could
be combined into buildings which
could deviate from the rather modest
high-rise on the box. (Vero used this
freedom and offered a Minol gas station in the form of a high-rise ground
floor.) Compared to the children's
game "The little big block builder,"
which was produced by "plapsi" from
1970 onward and which was made
up of individual pieces, both of the
Vero models were comparatively
inflexible. Each module generally
contained three floors, which meant
that the model height was limited to
multiples of three.

LINKS Der Vero-Bausatz „Wohnhausgruppe" mit dem „Raumzellen"-
System
LEFT The Vero models "Group
of apartment buildings" with the
"compartment" system

RECHTS Sanierte PH16-Häuser in
Erfurt am Juri-Gagarin-Ring und am
Johannesplatz
RIGHT Restored PH16 buildings in
Erfurt on Juri Gagarin Ring and at
Johannesplatz

DINA DOROTHEA FALBE

Nurda-Ferienhaus

NURDA VACATION HOUSE

MODELLBAUSATZ:
Nurda-Ferienhaus, B-262;
Maleratelier, B-255

MODEL ASSEMBLY KIT:
Nurda vacation house, B-262;
Painter's studio, B-255

PRODUKTIONSZEITRAUM:
1973 bis 1979 (B 261); 1979 bis
1984 (B-255)

PRODUCTION PERIOD:
1973 until 1979 (B-261); 1979
until 1984 (B-255)

HERSTELLER:
Gebr. Faller GmbH, Gütenbach
im Schwarzwald

MANUFACTURER:
Gebr. Faller GmbH, Gütenbach in
the Black Forest

MASSE:
13 x 10 x 6,5 cm

MEASUREMENTS:
13 x 10 x 6.5 cm

„Modern" ist vielleicht nicht das erste Wort, das einem bei einem Nurdachhaus in den Sinn kommt: ein befestigtes Zelt, ein steiles Satteldach, mehr eigentlich nicht. Es ist allerdings kein Zufall, dass dieser Haustyp ab den späten 1960er Jahren viele Ferienparks füllte – und in den 1970ern als Faller-Modell auch im bundesdeutschen Eigenheim vertreten war. Bevor das Prinzip „Fertighaus" für den Wohnungsbau üblich wurde, hatte es sich in den 1960er Jahren im boomenden Tourismus durchgesetzt. In der Angebotsfülle reüssierte die Firma Nurda (Architekten Ervenich/Immich, Wolfsburg/Berlin) um 1967 durch eine ikonische Form.

"Modern" is maybe not the first word that comes to mind for an A-frame house: a mounted tent, a steep pitched roof, not much more than that actually. It is, however, not a coincidence that this house type filled the vacation parks from the late 1960s onward—and was represented as a West German single family home in the 1970s as a Faller model. The principle of "prefabricated houses" gained influence in the booming tourism of the 1960s before it became common in housing construction. The company Nurda (Architects Ervenich/Immich, Wolfsburg/Berlin) rose to the top of the booming market around 1967 with their iconic form.

Trotz oder gerade wegen seiner innerdeutschen Grenzlage war der Harz eines der beliebtesten Urlaubsgebiete. Rund ein Viertel der Zweitwohnsitze zu Freizeitzwecken entfiel nach Edgar Fischer, der 1976 eine Forschungsarbeit zu diesem Thema veröffentlichte, auf Westberliner. Sie fanden hier einen nahgelegenen und zugleich bundesdeutschen Erholungsraum. „Mit 120 gemeldeten Wochenend- und Ferienhäusern dürfte Wolfshagen hinsichtlich des Bestandes an Freizeitwohnsitzen unter den Harzorten an der Spitze stehen", bemerkte Fischer. Nachdem hier erste Feriendomizile außergesetzlich entstanden waren, sollte eine neue Siedlung dafür einen geordneten Rahmen schaffen. Ab 1968 wurde ein etwa neun Hektar großes Hanggrundstück zwischen Dorf und Campingplatz abgegrenzt und einer von vier Abschnitten an die Firma Nurda vergeben. Der Bebauungsplan forderte naturnah gruppierte Häuser in „Zeltform" aus „Holz, Wellasbestzement und Beton für die Fundamente". Bis heute verweist hier ein blau glasierter „Grundstein" im gemauerten Sockel von Wolfshagener Nurda-Häusern identitätsstiftend auf das Jahr 1970.

Despite, or perhaps because of, its proximity to the internal German border, the Harz was one of the most well-loved vacation spots for West Germans. According to research by Edgar Fischer from 1976, about one quarter of all second homes for recreation located in the Harz were owned by West Berliners. In the Harz, they found a nearby and at the same time West German recreation area. "With 120 registered weekend and vacation houses, Wolfshagen is the location with the highest number of vacation properties in the Harz," wrote Fischer. After the first vacation homes were constructed here illegally, a new neighborhood was created to give this development an orderly framework. In 1968, a nine-hectare plot on a hill between the village and the camping grounds was split off and divided into four parts; one of these was assigned to the Nurda company. The construction permit required naturalistic groups of "tent-formed" houses made of "wood, corrugated asbestos cement, and concrete for the foundations." Up until today, a blue glazed "cornerstone" in the stone foundations of Nurda houses in Wolfshagen indicate the year 1970 and their identity.

Die Nurda-Siedlung in Wolfshagen
im Harz auf einer Postkarte der
1970er Jahre und heute
The Nurda estate in Wolfshagen in
the Harz region on a postcard from
the 1970s and today

Der allgemeine Siegeszug der Nurdach-Form weckte rasch das Interesse der Faller-Brüder. Man nahm Kontakt zum Anbieter Nurda auf und wurde sich handelseinig. 1973 kam das Nurda-Ferienhaus erstmals en miniature in den Katalog. Dass diese Bauform im Großen preisgünstig und ortsunabhängig funktionierte, machte sie modern. Man konnte sich vom Nachbarn abgrenzen, ohne auf ein anheimelndes Satteldach oder holzverkleidete Giebelseiten verzichten zu müssen. Inwiefern das Ferienhaus bald auch als ein Stück Freiheit galt, zeigt der Faller-Bausatz, der 1979 in ein Maleratelier umgewandelt wurde: Ein Dachfenster enthüllte den beleuchteten Rückzugsort männlicher Künstler mit weiblichen Aktmodellen. Damit war eine gewisse sexuelle Freizügigkeit bis in die beschauliche Miniaturwelt vorgedrungen.

The general success of the A-frame form quickly aroused the Faller brothers' interest. They contacted the Nurda company and reached an agreement. In 1973, the Nurda vacation house in miniature appeared in the catalog for the first time. The fact that this construction form worked well on a large scale inexpensively and in a variety of locations made it modern. One could distance oneself from the neighbors without having to go without a cozy pitched roof or wooden-sided gable ends. The Faller model also demonstrated the degree to which the vacation house acted as a form of freedom. In 1979, it was transformed into an artist's studio: a skylight reveals the illuminated retreat of the male artist and his female model. And with this, a certain amount of sexual freedom had made its way into the tranquil miniature world.

Das Faller-Modell „Maleratelier" mit den Preiser-Figuren des Künstlers und seiner Aktmodelle, abgebildet auch auf dem historischen Karton
The Faller model "Painter's studio" with the Preiser figures by the artist and his nude models, also depicted on the historical box

LINKS/RECHTS Ein Nurda-Ferienhaus
in Wolfshagen mit dazu passendem
Vogelhäuschen
LINKS/RIGHT A Nurda vacation house
in Wolfshagen with a matching
birdhouse

UNTEN Der „Grundstein" der Nurda-
Ferienhäuser in Wolfshagen mit der
Jahreszahl 1970
BELOW The "cornerstone" of a Nurda
vacation house in Wolfshagen with
the year inscription 1970

ANHANG APPENDIX

Biografien
BIOGRAPHIES

Daniel Bartetzko, *1969, Germanist M. A., Studium der Germanistik, Kunstgeschichte und Kulturanthropologie in Frankfurt am Main, 1998–2007 freier Journalist im Bereich Feuilleton unter anderem für die Frankfurter Rundschau, heute Redakteur bei den Zeitschriften Oldtimer Markt und Oldtimer Praxis, Mitherausgeber des Online-Magazins moderneREGIONAL.

Dr. Karin Berkemann, *1972, Diplom-Theologin, Kunsthistorikerin M. A., Fortbildung „Architekt in der Denkmalpflege", seit 2002 freie Kirchbau-Projekte, 2008–2010 wissenschaftliche Volontärin/Angestellte beim Landesamt für Denkmalpflege Hessen, heute Kustodin der Gustaf-Dalman-Sammlung/Lehrauftrag an der Universität Greifswald, Mitherausgeberin des Online-Magazins moderneREGIONAL.

Andreas Beyer, *1959, Studium der Germanistik und Kunstgeschichte in Frankfurt am Main, ab 1987 freier Journalist im Bereich Motorrad, seit Anfang der 1990er als Fotograf tätig, Schwerpunkte nun Reportage, Reise und Automobil, ab 2017 Bildbeiträge bei moderneREGIONAL.

Oliver Elser, *1972, Studium der Architektur in Berlin, Tätigkeiten als Kurator und Architekturkritiker, seit 2007 Kurator am Deutschen Architekturmuseum (DAM) Frankfurt am Main, unter anderem 2012 für die Ausstellung „Das Architekturmodell – Werkzeug, Fetisch, kleine Utopie" und 2016 für „Making Heimat" im Deutschen Pavillon auf der Architekturbiennale in Venedig.

Dina Dorothea Falbe, *1989, Architekturstudium in Weimar und Delft, freie Architekturjournalistin unter anderem für baunetz, Buchprojekt „Architekturen des Gebrauchs"

Daniel Bartetzko, *1969, M. A. German, studied German, art history, and cultural anthropology in Frankfurt am Main. 1998–2007 freelance journalist in the feature section for the Frankfurter Rundschau among others. Today editor of the magazines Oldtimer Markt and Oldtimer Praxis, co-editor of the online magazine moderneREGIONAL.

Dr. Karin Berkemann, *1972, diploma in theology, M. A. in art history, occupational training "Architect in Monument Preservation." Since 2002, independent church construction projects. 2008–2010 research volunteer/employee at the Hesse State Office for Monument Preservation. Today, curator of the Gustaf Dalman Collection, adjunct lecturer at the University of Greifswald, co-editor of the online magazine moderneREGIONAL.

Andreas Beyer, *1959, studied German and art history in Frankfurt am Main. Since 1987, freelance journalist for motorcycles. Since the beginning of the 1990s, work as a freelance photographer. Current focus commentary, travel and automobiles. Since 2017, image contributions to moderneREGIONAL.

Oliver Elser, *1972, studied architecture in Berlin. Worked as a curator and architecture critic. Since 2007, curator at the German Architecture Museum (DAM) in Frankfurt am Main, including the 2012 exhibition "Das Architekturmodell – Werkzeug, Fetisch, kleine Utopie" and the 2016 exhibition "Making Heimat" in the German pavilion at the architecture biennial in Venice.

Dina Dorothea Falbe, *1989, studied architecture in Weimar and Delft. Freelance architecture journalist, including for baunetz. Book project "Architekturen des Gebrauchs" (with

(mit Christopher Falbe), laufende Promotion zum Schulbau der DDR.

Teresa Fankhänel, Kuratorin am Architekturmuseum der TU München.

Christian Holl, Geschäftsführer des BDA Hessen, freier Autor, Mitherausgeber der Architekturplattform „marlowes,", Architekturstudium an der RWTH Aachen und der Universität Stuttgart, verschiedene Lehraufträge, 1997–2004 Redakteur der „db deutsche bauzeitung", seit 2008 im Ausstellungsausschuss/Kurator an der architekturgalerie am weißenhof e. V., Stuttgart.

Dr. Falk Jaeger, *1950, Studium der Architektur und Kunstgeschichte in Braunschweig, Stuttgart und Tübingen, ab 1976 Tätigkeit als Architekturkritiker, 2001–2002 Chefredakteur der „db deutsche bauzeitung", seit 2002 freier Publizist, Kritiker, Kurator und Juror, Lehraufträge unter anderem in Braunschweig und Dresden.

Ralf Liptau (promoviert), Studium der Kunst- und Architekturgeschichte in Berlin und Paris, 2014–2017 wissenschaftlicher Mitarbeiter am

Christopher Falbe). Currently completing a PhD about school architecture in the GDR.

Teresa Fankhänel, curator of the architecture museum at the TU Munich.

Christian Holl, managing director of the BDA Hesse. Freelance author. Co-editor of the architecture platform "marlowes,". Studied architecture at the RWTH Aachen and at the University of Stuttgart. Various adjunct teaching positions. 1997–2004 editor of "db deutsche bauzeitung." Since 2008, curator and member of the exhibition board at the architekturgalerie am weißenhof e. V., Stuttgart.

Dr. Falk Jaeger, *1950, studied architecture and art history in Braunschweig, Stuttgart and Tübingen. Since 1976, work as an architecture critic. 2001–2002 editor in chief of "db deutsche bauzeitung." Since 2002, freelance publicist, critic, curator, and juror. Adjunct lecturer in Braunschweig and Dresden.

Ralf Liptau (doctorate), studied art and architectural history in Berlin and Paris. 2014–2017 research

Graduiertenkolleg „Das Wissen der Künste" an der Universität der Künste Berlin, heute Universitätsassistent an der TU Wien, Promotionsprojekt zu Architekturmodellen in der Nachkriegsmoderne.

Dr. Matthias Ludwig, *1964, Studium von Bauingenieurwesen, Kunstgeschichte und Theologie, 1991–1996 wissenschaftlicher Mitarbeiter/2001–2007 Assistent am Marburger Kirchbauinstitut, 1999–2001 Projektbetreuer bei der Stiftung zur Bewahrung kirchlicher Baudenkmäler in Deutschland, heute freier Berater für neue Nutzungs- und Gestaltungskonzepte an Kirchengebäuden.

Leopold Messmer, *1928, Ausbildung zum Zimmermann, Studium der Architektur am Staatstechnikum Karlsruhe, einjähriges Praktikum bei Egon Eiermann, eigenes Architekturbüro in Furtwangen, Aufträge vorwiegend im Industriebau unter anderem für die Modellbaufirma Faller und den Uhrenhersteller Hanhart.

Verena Pfeiffer-Kloss, *1981, Dipl.-Ing. Stadt- und Regionalplanung, Studium an der TU Berlin,

employee at the graduate college "Das Wissen der Künste" at the University of Arts in Berlin. Today, university assistant at the Technical University in Vienna. Doctoral research about architectural models in post-war modernism.

Dr. Matthias Ludwig, *1964, studied civil engineering, art history, and theology. 1991–1996 research employee at the Marburg church construction institute. 1999–2001 project supervisor for the Foundation for the Preservation of Ecclesiastical Monuments in Germany. 2001–2007 assistant at the Marburg church construction institute. Today, freelance consultant for new use and design concepts for ecclesiastical buildings.

Leopold Messmer, *1928, training as a carpenter. Studied architecture at the Staatstechnikum Karlsruhe. One-year internship in the office of Egon Eiermann. Opened own architecture office in Furtwangen. Contracts primarily in industrial construction, including for the model building company Faller and the watchmaker Hanhart.

seit 2014 Akademische Mitarbeiterin im DFG-Graduiertenkolleg „Kulturelle und technische Werte historischer Bauten" an der BTU Cottbus, Lektorin beim JOVIS Verlag Berlin, Promotion zur nachkriegsmodernen U-Bahnarchitektur in Berlin, Vorstandsvorsitzende von urbanophil.

Dr. des. C. Julius Reinsberg, *1987, Historiker M. A., 2007–2012 Studium der Geschichtswissenschaften und Germanistik in Bonn und Gießen, bis 2017 Promotion am Lehrstuhl für Neueste Geschichte in Frankfurt am Main, heute Geschäftsführer der ernst-may-gesellschaft Frankfurt am Main, Mitherausgeber des Online-Magazins moderneREGIONAL.

Dr. Jörg Schilling, *1960, Studium der Kunstgeschichte und Geschichte in Hamburg, Promotion 2003, freier Kunsthistoriker, Autor, Kurator und Dozent, wissenschaftlicher Mitarbeiter der Martin-Elsaesser-Stiftung, Verleger und Inhaber des Schaff Verlags Hamburg, Vorsitzender der Karl Schneider Gesellschaft e. V.

Dr. Otto Schweitzer, *1950, Soziologiestudium in Wien und Frankfurt am Main, wissenschaftliche und

Verena Pfeiffer-Kloss, *1981, Dipl.-Ing. Urban and regional planning, TU Berlin. Since 2014 research employee for the DFG graduate college "Cultural and Technological Values of Historic Buildings" Berlin and Cottbus. Today editor at JOVIS Verlag Berlin. Doctoral project about post-war modernist architecture of subway stations in Berlin. Managing director of urbanophil.

Dr. des. C. Julius Reinsberg, *1987, M. A. in history. 2007–2012 studied history and German in Bonn and Gießen. Until 2017, doctoral research at the chair for modern history in Frankfurt am Main. Today managing director of the ernst-may-gesellschaft Frankfurt am Main, co-editor of the online magazine moderneREGIONAL.

Dr. Jörg Schilling, *1960, studied art history and history in Hamburg. Completed doctorate in 2003. Freelance art historian, author, curator, and lecturer. Research employee at the Martin-Elsaesser-Stiftung; Publicist and owner of the Schaff Verlag Hamburg, chairman of the Karl Schneider Gesellschaft e. V.

journalistische Tätigkeiten, ab 1990 selbstständige Filmprojekte zu soziologischen und pädagogischen, später auch zu (bau-)künstlerischen Themen, Filmografie mit über 60 Titeln, darunter zum Beispiel „Ernst May – eine Revolution des Großstädters" (2015).

Klaus Staeck, *1938, Jurastudium in Hamburg, Heidelberg und Berlin, 1965 Gründer des Produzentenverlags Edition Tangente (Edition Staeck), Rechtsanwalt, Gastdozenturen in Düsseldorf und Kassel, 2006–2015 Präsident der Akademie der Künste in Berlin, Grafiker, Plakatkünstler, schuf 1972 das Plakat „Deutsche Arbeiter! Die SPD will euch eure Villen im Tessin wegnehmen".

Hagen Stier, *1976, Architekturstudium in Hamburg, 2003–2008 Tätigkeit als angestellter Architekt in verschiedenen Architekturbüros in Hamburg, New York und Stockholm, seit 2009 freier Architekt in Hamburg, freier Architekturfotograf.

Dr. Otto Schweitzer, *1950, studied sociology in Vienna and Frankfurt am Main. Worked in research and journalism. From 1990 onward, freelance film projects about sociological and pedagogical, later also artistic and architectural, topics. Filmography with more than 60 titles, including for example "Ernst May – eine Revolution des Großstädters" (2015).

Klaus Staeck, *1938, studied law in Hamburg, Heidelberg and Berlin. 1965 founded the manufacturer publishing house Edition Tangente (Edition Staeck). Lawyer. Guest lecturer in Düsseldorf and Kassel. 2006–2015 president of the Academy of Arts in Berlin. Graphic designer. Poster artist. Designed the 1972 poster "German workers! The SPD wants to take away your villas in Ticino."

Hagen Stier, *1976, studied architecture in Hamburg. 2003–2008 employed as an architect in various architecture offices in Hamburg, New York and Stockholm. Since 2009, freelance architect in Hamburg and freelance architecture photographer.

Literaturauswahl
SELECTED LITERATURE

Alberti, Leon Battista, Zehn Bücher über die Baukunst, ins Deutsche übertragen, eingeleitet und mit Anmerkungen und Zeichnungen versehen durch Max Theuer, 4 Bde., Wien/Leipzig 1912.

Bahrdt, Hans P., Grundformen sozialer Situationen. Eine kleine Grammatik des Alltagslebens, hg. von Ulf Herlyn, München 1996.

Balcke, Gernot (Bearb.), Die schönsten Märklin Anlagen. 30 vorbildliche Anlagen in Baugröße H0 bis Z, Düsseldorf 1979.

Baumunk, Bodo-Michael, Der H0-Modell-Eisenbahner und seine Welt, Marburg 1985.

Benjamin, Walter, Das Kunstwerk im Zeitalter seiner technischen Reproduzierbarkeit. Drei Studien zur Kunstsoziologie (edition suhrkamp 28), Frankfurt am Main 1963.

Berger, Peter L./Luckmann, Thomas, Die gesellschaftliche Konstruktion der Wirklichkeit. Eine Theorie der Wissenssoziologie, Frankfurt am Main 1969.

Biene, Ulrich, Faller. Kleine Welt ganz groß, Bielefeld 2016.

Blumenberg, Hans, Theorie der Lebenswelt, Berlin 2010.

Braun, Frederik und Gerrit, Kleine Welt, großer Traum. Die Erfolgsgeschichte der Gründer des Miniatur Wunderlandes, Hamburg 2017.

Croy, Oliver/Elser, Oliver, Sondermodelle. Die 387 Häuser des Peter Fritz, Versicherungsbeamter aus Wien. Special Models (Katalog des Österreichischen Museums für Volkskunde 77), hg. von Franz Grieshofer, Ostfildern-Ruit 2001.

Durth, Werner/Gutschow, Niels, Nicht wegwerfen. Architektur und Städtebau der Fünfziger Jahre (Schriftenreihe des Deutschen Nationalkomitees für Denkmalschutz 33), Bonn 1987.

Etscheid, Georg, Kleine Weltmeister. Bausätze für eine heile Welt. Niemand trifft den Geschmack von Modellbaufans so genau wie der Familienbetrieb Faller, in: Die Zeit 51, 12. Dezember 2002.

Fischer, Edgar, Ferienwohnsitze im Harz, in: Neues Archiv für Niedersachsen 1976, 3, S. 221–240.

Fischer, Joseph, Chronik von Gütenbach, Uttenweiler 1904.

Giefer, Alois u. a. (Bearb.), Planen und Bauen in Deutschland, hg. vom Bund Deutscher Architekten (BDA), vom Deutschen Architekten- und Ingenieurverband (DAI) und vom Bund Deutscher Garten- und Landschaftsarchitekten, Wiesbaden (ursprünglich Köln/Opladen) 1960.

Grasskamp, Walter, Kleinmut. Hinweise zum Modell, in: Daidalos 26, 1987, S. 62–71.

Hahn, Renate und Otto (Hg.), Sonneberger Spielzeug – Made in Judenbach. 300 Jahre Spielzeugherstellung an der alten Handelsstraße (Studien zur Volkskunde in Thüringen), Münster in Westfalen/New York 2010.

Hill, Joachim M., Modellbahn Gleispläne. 100 Ideen für kleine und große Anlagen (alba modellbahn praxis 1), 2. Auflage, Düsseldorf 1982.

Holl, Christian, Zeichen der Zeit. Der Bonner Kanzlerbungalow und das Bundesviertel im Kontext von Alltäglichkeit, in: Vergegenwärtigung. Erinnerung, Inszenierung, Spekulation, hg. von der Wüstenrot Stiftung, Ludwigsburg 2014, S. 49–57.

Just, Marcel/Speiser, Meret, Der Traum von Amerika. 50er-Jahre-Bauten in den Alpen, Katalog, 11. September – 20. November 2016, Nidwaldner Museum Salzmagazin, Stans/Schweiz 2016.

Kiegeland, Burkhardt, Modelleisenbahn. Ein Hand- und Spielbuch, München u. a. 1975.

Kirschbaum, Juliane/Viebrock, Jan (Bearb.), Architektur und Städtebau der Fünf-

ziger Jahre. Am 30. und 31. August 1988. Beiträge vom 14. Hessischen Tag für Denkmalpflege am 8. und 9. September 1988 in Darmstadt (Dokumentation der Pressefahrt des Deutschen Nationalkomitees für Denkmalschutz 14; Schriftenreihe des Deutschen Nationalkomitees für Denkmalschutz 36), Bonn 1988.

Knaden, Martin (Bearb.), Stadt-Bahn (MIBA SPEZIAL 68), Nürnberg 2006.

Liptau, Ralf, Häuser im Herbarium. Medien der Architekturvermittlung am Beispiel der Internationalen Bauausstellung 1957, in: wissenskuenste.de 3, November 2014. https://wissenderkuenste.de/texte/ausgabe-3/haeuser-im-herbarium-medien-der-architekturvermittlung-am-beispiel-der-internationalen-bauausstellung-1957, 11. November 2017.

Modellbau leicht gemacht, H0 N (Faller 841), Gütenbach im Schwarzwald o. J. [ca. 1981].

Mosebach, Martin, Und wir nennen diesen Schrott auch noch schön. Wider das heutige Bauen, in: Frankfurter Allgemeine Zeitung, 28. Juni 2010.

Spinnen, Burkhard, Kleine Philosophie der Passionen. Modelleisenbahn, München 1998.

Steets, Silke, Der sinnhafte Aufbau der gebauten Welt. Eine Architektursoziologie, Berlin 2015.

Stein, Bernhard (Bearb.), Gleisanlagen nach dem Vorbild – mit Entwürfen für die Baugrößen H0 N (Faller 844), Gütenbach/Schwarzwald o. J. [1980].

Tesch, Sebastian, Albert Speer (1905–1981) (Hitlers Architekten 2), Wien u. a. 2016.

Vale, Brenda und Robert Vale, Architecture on the carpet. The curious tale of construction toys and the genesis of modern buildings, Lodon 2013.

Verfürth, Werner, Die Gaststätte im Gocher Bahnhof, in: An Niers und Kendel Juli 2011, S. 1–11.

Wagenbrenner, Amadus, Kirchenführer der Kath. Pfarrkirche St. Katharina Gütenbach im Schwarzwald, hg. vom Katholischen Pfarramt Gütenbach, Saarbrücken 2000.

Internetquellen
INTERNET SOURCES

Internetauftritt von Conrad antiquario mit Katalogarchiv u. a., http://www.conradantiquario.de, 24. März 2018.

Internetauftritt des Künstlers Rainer Dorwarth, http://www.dorwarth.com, 11. November 2017.

Internetportal Forschungsprojekt Architektur und Ingenieurbaukunst der 1950er, 60er und 70er Jahre in NRW, TU Dortmund, http://www.nrw-architekturdatenbank. tu-dortmund.de, 26. März 2018.

Online-Forum Alte Modellbahnen, http://alte-modellbahnen.xobor.de, 24. März 2018.

Zeitschriften
JOURNALS

1000 Möglichkeiten mit Vollmer Teilen, Faller Modellbau Magazin (später: Welt der Modellbahn), Märklin-Magazin, Modellbahn Praxis, Der Modelleisenbahner.

Modellbau- und Modellbahnkataloge
MODELMAKING CATALOGS

Auhagen, Eheim, Faller, Fleischmann, Kibri, Märklin, Noch, Owo, Piko, Preiser, Dr. Rudolf Spitaler, Trix, VauPe, Vollmer, Wiad, Wiking, Zeuke.

Archive/Materialien
ARCHIVES/MATERIALS

Auktionshaus Bergstraße, Weinheim; Siegfried Armbruster, Gütenbach im Schwarzwald; Thomas Balzer, Berlin; Archiv Daniel Bartetzko, Frankfurt am Main; Baukunstarchiv, Akademie der Künste, Berlin; Friedrich Baumer, Gütenbach im Schwarzwald; Ulrich Biene, Rüthen; Bundesarchiv, Koblenz; Gebr. Faller GmbH, Gütenbach im Schwarzwald; Guscetti Architetti, Minusio; Hier & jetzt am Turmcafé, Freiburg im Breisgau; Marcel Just, Zürich; Landesarchiv Thüringen, Staatsarchiv Meiningen, Archivdepot Suhl; Stephan Lippmann, Pockau; Architekturbüro Ferdinand Merkenthaler, Freiburg im Breisgau; Architekturbüro Poldi Messmer, Furtwangen; Nurda-Hausbau GmbH, Burgwedel-Großburgwedel; Stadt Badenweiler, Bauamt; Stadtarchiv Goch; Viessmann Modelltechnik GmbH, Hatzfeld; Wirtschaftsarchiv Baden-Württemberg, Stuttgart.

Bildnachweis
PHOTO CREDITS

Seiten pages 8, 21, 27, 29–32, 39, 42, 57, 72, 116 oben top, 122: Vorlagen (historische Kataloge und Kartons) templates (historical catalogs and boxes): Privatarchiv private archive Daniel Bartetzko, Frankfurt am Main; Seiten pages 10, 12, 22–23, 37, 70, 73–76, 79–86, 89–92, 95–98, 99 rechts right, 100, 103–106, 109, 110 oben top, 111–112, 115, 116 unten bottom, 117–118, 121, 123–125, 136, Vor-/Nachsatzpapier endpapers (Faller-Hochhaus Faller high-rise, Gütenbach im Schwarzwald): Hagen Stier, Hamburg; Seite page 19: Bundesarchiv Bild 146-1979-178-17; Seiten pages 25, 35, 44, 64–67: Andreas Beyer, Wiesbaden; Seite page 36: Wirtschaftsarchiv Baden-Württemberg, Stuttgart; Seite page 28: Vorlage template: Conrad antiquario. Berlin; Seiten pages 47–48, 59: Standbild screenshot, Begleitfilm zur Ausstellung accompanying movie for the exhibition, Otto Schweitzer/C. Julius Reinsberg; Seite page 49 links left: Edition Staeck, Heidelberg; Seite page 49 rechts right: Baukunstarchiv, Akademie der Künste, Berlin, wohl frühe 1960er Jahre probably in the early 1960s; Seite page 52: Elmar Herr, Kissingen; Seite page 54: Bundesarchiv B 145 Bild F074647-0019; Seite page 60–61: Privatarchiv private archive Falk Jaeger, Berlin; Seite page 78: Aldo (Architekt architect) und and Alberto (Ingenieur engineer) Guscetti, Villa Giovanni Guscetti, Ambrì-Piotta, 1958, Foto photo: Willi Borelli, Airolo, Archiv Guscetti Architetti, Minusio; Seite page 88: Privatarchiv private archive Hier & jetzt am Turmcafé, Freiburg im Breisgau; Seiten pages 94, 99 links left: Privatarchiv private archive Friedrich Baumer, Gütenbach im Schwarzwald; Seite page 102: Stadtarchiv Goch, Sammlung Weinrother; Seiten pages 108, 110 unten bottom: Badische Zeitung (Markgräfler Nachrichten) 144, 26. Juni 1963, Seite page 9, Foto photo: Franz Josef Mayer, Vorlage template: Archiv Bauamt, Bürgermeisteramt Badenweiler; Seite page 114: Postkarte postcard, Auslese-Bild-Verlag, Bad Salzungen, frühe 1970er Jahre in the early 1970s; Seite page 120: Postkarte postcard, Kunstanstalt Carl Thoericht, Hann. Münden, wohl 1970er Jahre probably in the 1970s.

Danksagung
ACKNOWLEDGEMENTS

Architekturbüro Ferdinand Merkenthaler, Freiburg im Breisgau
Architekturbüro Poldi Messmer, Furtwangen
Siegfried Armbruster, Gütenbach im Schwarzwald
Augsburger Puppenkiste, Augsburg
Auhagen GmbH, Marienberg im Erzgebirge
Auktionshaus Bergstraße, Weinheim
Thomas Balzer, Berlin
Baukunstarchiv, Akademie der Künste, Berlin
Friedrich Baumer, Gütenbach im Schwarzwald
Ulrich Biene, Rüthen
Bundesarchiv, Koblenz
Conrad antiquario, Berlin
Tino Celio, Ambrì im Tessin
Deutsche Bahn, Frankfurt am Main
Edition Staeck, Heidelberg
Familie Thielen-Schwintek, Frankfurt am Main
Familien Neidhard und Sauer, Gütenbach im Schwarzwald
Gaststätte zum Bahnhof, Goch
Gebr. Faller GmbH, Gütenbach im Schwarzwald
Gebr. Märklin & Cie. GmbH, Göppingen
Gerald Fuchs, Kaufbeuren
Guscetti Architetti, Minusio
Hamburgisches Architekturarchiv, Hamburg
Elmar Herr, Kissingen
hier & jetzt am Turmcafé, Freiburg im Breisgau
Marcel Just, Zürich
Katholische Kirche im Bregtal

Christina Kersten, Braunschweig
Jim Knopf, Lummerland
Stefan Kock, Frankfurt am Main
Cirsten Körner, Frankfurt am Main
Christian Kyrieleis, Frankfurt am Main
Landesarchiv Thüringen, Staatsarchiv Meiningen, Archivdepot Suhl
Stephan Lippmann, Pockau
Literarisches Museum Badenweiler „Tschechow-Salon"
Wiebke Meyer, Eisighofen
Miniatur Wunderland, Hamburg
Bernd Mittländer, Frankfurt am Main
Nurda-Haushau GmbH, Burgwedel-Großburgwedel
Marion del Pozo, Frankfurt am Main
Schaff Verlag, Hamburg
Stadt Badenweiler
Stadt Goch
Startnext Crowdfunding GmbH, Dresden
Alle Unterstützende der Crowdfunding-Aktion zum Film zur Ausstellung
Viessmann Modelltechnik GmbH, Hatzfeld
Wirtschaftsarchiv Baden-Württemberg, Stuttgart
Wüstenrot Stiftung, Ludwigsburg

Impressum
IMPRINT

Ausstellung
EXHIBITION

märklinMODERNE
Vom Bau zum Bausatz und zurück
From architecture to assembly kit and back again

19. Mai–9. September 2018 May 19–September 9, 2018

Eine Ausstellung des Online-Magazins moderneREGIONAL
An exhibition by the online magazine moderneREGIONAL

Direktor DAM Director DAM: Peter Cachola Schmal
Stellvertretende Direktorin DAM Deputy Director DAM: Andrea Jürges
Kurator DAM Curator DAM: Oliver Elser
Kuratoren der Ausstellung Exhibition curators: Daniel Bartetzko
und and Karin Berkemann
Modell- und Architekturfotografie Model and architecture photography: Hagen Stier
Porträtfotografie Portrait photography: Andreas Beyer
Begleitfilm Accompanying movie: Otto Schweitzer, C. Julius Reinsberg
Ausstellungsdesign Exhibition design: Mario Lorenz, Deserve Wiesbaden
Aufbau/Installation Team Assembly/installation team: Marina Barry, Paolo Brunino, Ulrich
Diekmann, Enrico Hirsekorn, Jannik Hoffmann, Caroline Krause, Ömer Simsek, Beate
Voigt, Gerhard Winkler unter der Leitung von under the direction of Christian Walter
Registrar: Wolfgang Welker
Führungen Guided tours: Yorck Förster
Architekturvermittlung Architecture presentation/education: Bettina Gebhardt, Jorma
Foth, Julia Reich, Frank Reinecke, Sonja Sikora, Hana Spijkers, Arne Winkelmann,
Michèle Zeuner, Anne Etheber, Karla Pohl unter der Leitung von under the direction of
Christina Budde

DAM Corporate Design: Gardeners, Frankfurt am Main
Öffentlichkeitsarbeit Public relations: Brita Köhler, Rebekka Rass
Sekretariat und Verwaltung Secretarial and administration: Inka Plechaty,
Jacqueline Brauer
Haustechnik Building technician: Joachim Müller-Rahn
Druck Printing: Inditec, Bad Camberg

Herausgeber Editors moderneREGIONAL:
Daniel Bartetzko, Karin Berkemann, C. Julius Reinsberg

märklinMODERNE wird gefördert durch die Wüstenrot Stiftung.
märklinMODERNE is sponsored by the Wüstenrot Stiftung.

© 2018 by jovis Verlag GmbH

Das Copyright für die Texte liegt bei den AutorInnen.
Das Copyright für die Abbildungen liegt bei den FotografInnen/InhaberInnen der Bildrechte.
Text by kind permission of the authors.
Pictures by kind permission of the photographers/holders of the picture rights.

Alle Rechte vorbehalten.
All rights reserved.

Umschlagmotiv Cover: Fotomontage von Hagen Stier mit seinen Aufnahmen der Villa Hermann Faller in Gütenbach im Schwarzwald (1961, Leopold Messmer), des Faller-Modells „Villa im Tessin" (seit 1961) und der Villa Giovanni Guscetti in Ambrì im Tessin (1958, Aldo und Alberto Guscetti)
Cover image: photomontage by Hagen Stier with his shots of Villa Hermann Faller in Gütenbach in the Black Forest (1961, Leopold Messmer), the Faller model "Villa in Ticino" (since 1961) and Villa Giovanni Guscetti in Ambri in Ticino (1958, Aldo and Alberto Guscetti)

Bibliografische Information der Deutschen Nationalbibliothek
Die Deutsche Nationalbibliothek verzeichnet diese Publikation in der deutschen Nationalbibliografie; detaillierte bibliografische Daten sind im Internet über http://dnb.d-nb.de abrufbar.
Bibliographic information published by the Deutsche Nationalbibliothek
The Deutsche Nationalbibliothek lists this publication in the Deutsche Nationalbibliografie; detailed bibliographic data are available on the Internet at http://dnb.d-nb.de.

jovis Verlag GmbH
Kurfürstenstraße 15/16
10785 Berlin
www.jovis.de

jovis-Bücher sind weltweit im ausgewählten Buchhandel erhältlich. Informationen zu unserem internationalen Vertrieb erhalten Sie von Ihrem Buchhändler oder unter www.jovis.de.
jovis books are available worldwide in select bookstores. Please contact your nearest bookseller or visit www.jovis.de for information concerning your local distribution.

ISBN 978-3-86859-518-5

Katalog
CATALOG

Diese Publikation erscheint anlässlich der Ausstellung
This publication is issued to accompany the exhibition

märklinMODERNE
Vom Bau zum Bausatz und zurück
From architecture to assembly kit and back again

19. Mai–9. September 2018 May 19–September 9, 2018

Eine Ausstellung des Online-Magazins moderneREGIONAL in und mit dem Deutschen Architekturmuseum
An exhibition by the online magazine moderneREGIONAL at and with the German Architecture Museum

Herausgeber Editors: Karin Berkemann, Daniel Bartetzko
Korrektorat (dt.) Proofreading (Ger.): jovis: Theresa Hartherz
Übersetzung Translation: Dr. Mary Dellenbaugh
Korrektorat (engl.) Proofreading (Eng.): Lynne Kolar-Thompson
Gestaltungskonzept Design concept: Jutta Drewes
Gestaltung und Satz Design and setting: jovis: Susanne Rösler
Lithografie Lithography: Bild1Druck, Berlin
Architektur- und Modellfotografie (soweit nicht anders angegeben)
Architecture and model photography (unless specified otherwise): Hagen Stier
Porträtfotografie (soweit nicht anders angegeben)
Portrait photography (unless specified otherwise): Andreas Beyer

Gedruckt in der Europäischen Union Printed in the European Union